Wilhelm Ru

The Ring o

Wilhelm Ruprecht Frieling

The Ring of the Nibelung

A retelling of Richard Wagner's opera

internet-Buchverlag.de

Imprint

Wilhelm Ruprecht Frieling
tells the story of Richard Wagner's scenic festival
The Ring of the Nibelung
© Wilhelm Ruprecht Frieling
www.RuprechtFrieling.de
Internet-Buchverlag, English Edition September 2015
www.Internet-Buchverlag.de
Translation: Dr. Claudia Rapp
www.claudiarapp.de
Artwork: Casandra Krammer
www.casandrakrammer.de
Illustrations: Hugo L. Braune
Layout: Michael Beautemps
www.buch-und-buch.de

The author welcomes praise, criticism and suggestions for improvement: frieling@aol.com

All rights reserved. No part of this publication may be reproduced, distributed, or transmitted in any form or by any means, including photocopying, recording, or other electronic or mechanical methods, without the prior written permission of the publisher, except in the case of brief quotations embodied in critical reviews and certain other noncommercial uses permitted by copyright law.durch Rundfunk, Fernsehen oder Video (auch einzelner Text- und Bildteile) sowie der Übersetzung in andere Sprachen.

Contents

Preface: An Opera Listener's Guide to the Underbelly of Wagner — 13

RHINEGOLD — 17
  Characters in the "Rhinegold" — 18
  Sex & Crime on the Rhine
  (SCENE ONE) — 19
  Gamblers on the Mountain of the Gods
  (SCENE TWO) — 26
  The Nibelheim Heist
  (SCENE THREE) — 34
  The Curse of the Ring
  (SCENE FOUR) — 38

THE VALKYRIE — 45
  Characters in "The Valkyrie" — 46

ACT ONE — 47
  Manhunt in the Forest
  (PRELUDE) — 47
  In the Enemy's House
  (SCENE ONE) — 48
  Hunding Appears
  (SCENE TWO) — 50
  Fateful One-Night Stand
  (SCENE THREE) — 54

ACT TWO — 60
  A Marital Quarrel in Wallhall
  (PRELUDE AND SCENE ONE) — 60
  Wotan's Confession
  (SCENE TWO) — 64

On the Run
(SCENE THREE) 70
Brünnhilde Defies her Orders
(SCENE FOUR) 71
Siegmund's Death
(SCENE FIVE) 74

ACT THREE 77
The Ride of the Valkyries
(PRELUDE AND SCENE ONE) 77
Wotan Casts out Brünnhilde
(SCENE TWO) 81
The Ordeal
(SCENE THREE) 83

SIEGFRIED 87
Characters in "Siegfried" 88

ACT ONE 89
The Smithy in the Forest
(PRELUDE) 89
The Foster Son of the Dwarf
(SCENE ONE) 90
A Life-or-Death Wager (Scene Two) 95
The Magical Sword
(SCENE THREE) 100

ACT TWO 106
The Ring Wanders on
(PRELUDE) 106
In front of the Cave of Envy
(SCENE ONE) 107
The Battle with the Dragon
(SCENE TWO) 109

The Ring Claims its Next Victim
(SCENE THREE)   115

ACT THREE   118
Strife at Valkyrie Rock
(PRELUDE)   118
Wotan Determines his End
(SCENE ONE)   118
Wotan's Power Shatters
(SCENE TWO)   121
The Lady in the Ocean of Fire
(SCENE THREE)   124
All's Well that Ends Well?   127

TWILIGHT OF THE GODS   129
Characters in "Twilight of the Gods"   130
Brünnhilde Receives the Ring
(PRELUDE)   131

ACT ONE   136
Siegfried's Journey on the Rhine
(SCENE ONE)   136
Blood Brotherhood
(SCENE TWO)   138
The Woman on the Rock is Captured
(SCENE THREE)   143

ACT TWO   149
The Nibelung's Plan
(SCENE ONE)   149
Siegfried Returns
(SCENE TWO)   151
Hagen Invites a Wedding
(SCENE THREE)   153

Brünnhilde Loses it (SCENE FOUR)	155
The Murder Conspiracy (SCENE FIVE)	162
ACT THREE	165
The Death Message from the Rhine (SCENE ONE)	165
Siegfried's Death (SCENE TWO)	168
Farewell to the Ring (SCENE THREE)	171
The Author	177

My worldview has found its most consummate artistic expression in the Ring. *It is the highest and most perfect thing that could spring from my pen and my powers.*

Richard Wagner to Franz Liszt, May 31, 1852

The Ring *has become the work of a lifetime, the work by which this artist will be remembered. It is the Song of Songs of German Idealism. In an admirable gesture that combines vigor and beauty, the poet-composer tears away the glittering mask from the face of the perniciously materialistic spirit of the present day, revealing the jeering face of the devil. His aim is to hammer into the hearts of the listeners the longing for liberation from this demon. The esthetic effect of the work of art is meant to be transformed into an ethic one; the viewer shall not only be uplifted, but also bettered. Wagner's intent is two-fold, both religious and artistic. This puts his creation in a line with the greatest works of the past. The noble goals he envisions connect the* Ring *with the Greek drama of the great tragedians, and with the mystery plays of the Middle Ages. The* Ring *was a magnificent exhortation for a world that was drowning in materialism. It was an avowal incarnate, and it is not Wagner's fault that people did not recognize this quality in his work.*

Max von Boehn: The Nibelung in Art, 1923

One Ring to rule them all,
One Ring to find them,
One Ring to bring them all
and in the darkness bind them

J. R. R. Tolkien: The Lord of the Rings 1954

Preface: An Opera Listener's Guide to the Underbelly of Wagner

The theft of the Rhinegold unleashes everything that has kept the world in suspense (and made it go round) until the present day: unfettered greed, boundless love, unfathomable hatred, consuming envy, the everlasting fight for personal freedom. Antipodes clash in battle: humans and gods, dwarves and giants, ethereal beings and thunderous forces of nature.

Richard Wagner, whose bicentenary birthday was celebrated worldwide in the "Wagner year" of 2013, created the most monumental "total work of art" of opera history with his four-part *Ring of the Nibelung*. Both the basic premise of the revolutionary stage play and its message are timely: The curse that ruins humankind is founded on the irresistible appeal of possession and the power invested in capital.

In the face of entire communities of states that rumble, crumble and then break apart, is it really necessary to expound on the topicality of this theme? Don't we see our own Walhall go up in flames on a daily basis? This inferno doesn't just turn money into ashes-basic human values are consumed by the flames as well. What about our regard for life and our respect for our neighbor? Gone with the backdraft.

It is a paradox of our times that the buzzword of the "Myth of Bayreuth" draws predominantly the representatives of *those* social classes which ignore the basic premise of the *Ring*, and precisely out of petty class interest. They perceive the opera with a sort of tunnel vision, indulging in the inebriation the music provides. And yet in his libretto, the composer devoted himself to the highest and most pressing issues, setting up unmistakable warning signs that were meant to tell us where we were headed.

Bearing this aspect in mind, the fact that young people today demand a fresh perspective on Richard Wagner's oeuvre should be seen as cause for hope. They are genuinely interested in the "underbelly of Wagner," and rightly so.

The *Ring of the Nibelung* is a young, very contemporary play, which becomes obvious once it is translated into current lingo. This *Ring* is so loaded with powerful eloquence and linguistic wit that it has the potential to blow one's socks off, if only the reader is willing to embark on the text. Wagner's prose is filled to the brim with funny, crisp allusions and references. At the same time it generates a dramatic pull that has the power to enthrall and captivate the attentive reader.

Wagner wrote his text before he started composing the music. He valued his "tetralogic poem" so much that he did a public reading of the complete and entire *Ring*, and published its text in 1853 in a small print edition at his own expense. He was well aware of both the explosive textual force and the poetic significance of his work. Contrary to the vast majority of all opera composers, he wrote all the texts to his operas himself, placing central importance on the words.

Contemporary critics like to dissect and diss his literary work, diverting attention away from its topicality by reducing Wagner to his music. They are fond of pointing out the plethora of old-fashioned words and phrasings, which the author employed to create a sense of a medieval, Middle Earth world.

Of course it is true that the original libretto is difficult to read if you don't happen to be in possession of the 33-volume German Lexicon by the Brothers Grimm, or some extensive Middle High German dictionary. Even the available English translations tend to sound dated and dry, taking their cue from the original, but missing its alliterative force.

This listener's guide is another type of translation, one that turns the difficult artificial language of Wagner into our everyday speech, while still pointing out the composer's idiosyncrasies and witticisms. It is a retelling of the dramatic plot along the lines of the libretto, which also draws connections to the music where significant. Its aim is to cut a path through the tangled underbrush of Wagner's story of the events surrounding the ring of the Nibelung, so a younger audience can find its way, and come to appreciate Wagner today.

Wilhelm Ruprecht Frieling

RHINEGOLD

Eve of the scenic festival *The Ring of the Nibelung*

First performance:
Munich, Königliches Hof- und Nationaltheater
September 22, 1869

Characters in the "Rhinegold"

Woglinde, Wellgunde, Flosshilde, the so-called Rhine daughters, supposed to guard the Rhinegold at the behest of their father, the river Rhine himself.

Alberich, Nibelung, leader of the black elves that live in the subterranean dwarf kingdom Nibelheim. He longs for love, is turned on and played for a fool by the Rhine daughters, and then steals the Rhinegold.

Mime, Alberich's brother, a skillful black- and goldsmith, suffers under Alberich's brutal regiment.

Wotan, boss of the god squad and unscrupulous potentate, tries to hold on to the reins both in heaven and on earth.

Fricka, goddess of marriage and morals, wants to keep her husband Wotan in check and keep him from straying.

Freia, goddess of youth, grows the precious apples that promise eternal youth in her orchard.

Donner, god of violence and anger, like to hit stuff with his heavy hammer.

Froh, as his German name implies, is the happy-go-lucky god of cheerfulness, a brother of Donner and Freia.

Loge may be only a demigod, but he muddles around in each and any of the extant worlds, and he loves plotting intrigues.

Fasolt and Fafner, two giants, are contracted by Wotan to build the mighty castle Walhall for the gods, only to be fleeced of their promised payment.

Erda, seer and mother of wisdom, warns Wotan of the consequences of his actions, and predicts the twilight of the gods.

Sex & Crime on the Rhine
(SCENE ONE)

This is where the world begins. Everything is in flow. Richard Wagner, the creator of this four-story opera *The Ring of the Nibelung* makes that crystal clear by putting 136 long beats into the orchestra's prelude to "Rhinegold." The overture is in E flat major, the key that his colleague Hector Berlioz had deemed majestic, sweet and haunting.

In Wagner's opus, ancient Father Rhine represents the significance of the life-giving elixir. Nature and life itself develop in the water. Oceans and rivers symbolize the cradle of all things. On this level, the world is in its initial stage, these are its origins. And thus, mythic music is played. The horns give us softly swaying arpeggios, the E flat major triad of E flat—G flat—B flat, before the celli and violins set in. We experience a musical creation poem. The events we are witness to once served to separate Good and Evil in our imagination.

Calmly the dark double basses open the prelude. Their low-pitched, steaming triad wafts up from the orchestra pit, followed by the bassoons, and then the horns weave themselves into the fabric of sound. Movement begins to grow out of the initial calm, expressed by spherical strings. This is the motif of coming into being, becoming, which is taken up by more instruments. The swaying, undulating and surging becomes livelier. Flooding figures of quavers/eights [Brit/Amer.] turn into sparkling, leaping semi-quavers/sixteenths. The river runs, the stream rushes, the flood rises from the deepest depths. It is as if the music carries the listener up from abysmal darkness up into the gleaming, blinding light.

Night on the Rhine. Riverscape with women. Water. Waves, awash. A milky mellow moon over this midsummer's night. Green, blue and silver. Must be the ideal moment for a peaceful bath. Magic moments awaken the spirit and body. But beauty is only skin-deep. As is peace, it seems.

Three young women are taking a bath in the refreshing waters. Their breasts are firm, their buttocks smooth, and their long hair shimmers just like silk. They're obviously in their element, the way they play and levitate in the tide, laughing and joking together. The refreshing bath renders them even more desirable than they already are—a wet dream come true. And each of these girls is fully aware of that fact, and of their effect.

Woglinde, Wellgunde and Flosshilde are sisters. Their old-fashioned names are their grizzled Daddy's fault: The Rhine is their father, and the Rhine is their home. Father Rhine begat three girls with the original mother Erda, also called Wala in her function as seer from Hel, the realm of the dead. As with many legendary sirings, this one supposedly did not come about because daddy was horny and mommy was feeling wild. No, there were foreboding and purpose involved, because the three sisters became the designated guardians of the treasure. Their task was to guard the Rhinegold slumbering deep down on the bottom of the river. That is their calling and their burden, their parental legacy.

So the three chicks live in that body of water; it truly is their element. While we may imagine the river's godfather as a wrinkled old graybeard, who is rumored to dabble in playing the lute, his daughters are vivacious and young enough to be jailbait. Teenagers, Nymphs, Lolitas, sexy as hell.

And some Humbert has already caught the bait. An abominable thing is lurking in the deep morass of the river, spying on the nymphs. A Peeping Tom, the case is clear! The girls are his private eye candy. He has been here before, he knows their habits, knows when to be on the lookout for them. They haunt his inappropriate dreams and make him come back to the river, over and over again. He cannot stop thinking about their bodies. If only he could be close to one of them, could touch her, smell her, lick her. He would give anything for a chance at that.

The voluptuary's name is Alberich. He's a dwarf, drawn out from underneath the earth by the lively splish-splashing going on. But his chances are minuscule. He's dirty and hasn't been groomed or washed in ages. On top of that, a pronounced lack of self-reflection, or maybe he is simply missing a mirror: mildewed skin, shaggy mane, matted robe. He does not even realize that he's drooling from his drooping lips. He pants and crawls like a wounded animal. To sum it up, he is a miserable creep who reeks of garbage and dump. Hasn't seen soap, brush or sponge in ages. The poor sod hiding in the dregs of the river is such an obvious no-go for any remotely pretty thing, anyone who watches the scene unfold knows right away: A nobody is trying to get fresh with the dewy nymphs.

The lovely trio knows full well that they are being watched. The daughters of the Rhine amuse themselves by luring the guy to witness their bathing spree. Their daily routine in the river is uniform enough as to make them desire variety. They have often tried to lure the shy worm up to the surface and into the light. To turn his head, of course. After a long hiatus, he's finally crawled out from his dark den in the deep again, and it looks as if he might venture from his boggy cover. Sometimes, drives and desires can be overwhelming. And speak of the devil, there he is, Alberich the sinister gnome!

Alberich is a black elf, a prince of hell and demon of the dark side, and at the same time he is the Lord of the Nibelung, that long-forgotten breed from the depths of the earth. In the feudal songs of the early Middle Ages, they were said to prospect for coal and iron ore, but also gold and diamonds. Other sources claimed that the Nibelungm were extremely averse to light (in other words: shady), and thus eager to lay their hands on anything that glistened and glittered. Among Wagnerians, discussions as to whether the house of the Nibelung still exists are rekindled with increasing regularity, similar to the tabloid accounts of sightings of the Loch Ness monster during slow news time. Deep waters are, as we all know, not merely deep but also murky.

The Nibelungs' abode is called Nibelheim. Though the name may have a homey, cozy ring to it, in reality it is an inhospitable, forbidding place. The few visitors that ventured down there and were lucky enough to re-emerge on the well-lit surface of the earth again had nothing even remotely inviting to report. They spoke of a maze of tubes and tunnels, of moldy chambers and damp bowers. It's icy cold down there, constantly dripping, and dotted with fierce volcanic fires. Sulfurous smell and coal dust tarnish the air. Nibelheim is not on anyone's bucket list; you won't find it in any tourist brochure.

The residents of Nibelheim are creatures of the underworld, who like daylight about as much as the devil likes holy water. Nobody is very keen on meeting them. Everyone is relieved if they can pass them by unscathed. And Alberich, our Peeping Tom, is a literal *untermensch*: Not only does he hail from the absolute basement of the earth, his thinking is also quite obviously governed by his nether regions. Psychologists like to label the species they analyze, and their tags are not always benevolent. They would probably describe Alberich as a guy who relies on his phallic GPS. In other words, he is dick-driven.

The pretty Woglinde doesn't need fatherly advice to understand this; her feminine instincts tell her. The Rhine daughter lures the lecherous old codger with her prettiest soprano voice. And it works, because Alberich is horny.

As soon as the troubadour grabs the girl however, she slips from his greedy grasp, utters a lascivious laugh, and then proceeds to taunt him from just out of reach. Alberich is clumsy in the wet element, slithers over slippery rocks, creeps and crawls after her, but is unable to catch her.

Now her sister Wellgunde approaches and offers herself to the lecher. Alberich is immediately taken with her, wooing the second soprano with his own, coaxing bass: *Twine your slender arms around me that I may toy and touch your neck and with ardent caress nestle against your soft breast.*

Who could resist such lyrical protestations of desire? Alas, his second attempt at wooing is as doomed to failure as his first. When he comes closer, the Rhine daughter No. 2 starts to abuse the smelly midget, calling him a hairy, humpbacked horror, and turns tail.

The oldest of the three, Flosshilde, is the most mature, sensible one. If she decides to join in the game with the strange suitor, she must be bored out of her mind. And here she goes, ensnaring Alberich in her alto web of pretty words, soft-soaping him like an expert barber, or the womanly woman that she is. Oh, how graceful he suddenly seems in her eyes; how encouraging his docile smile—in short: *Dearest of men!* If only he favored her ... And sure enough, the enchanted man warbles back at her: *Sweetest of maids! I'd hold you forever!*

He wants to grab what's his, but it turns out, he's fallen for yet another voluptuous vision. The devil from Nibelheim is forced to listen to a new tirade on his bristly beard, his wiry hair, and his croaking toad voice. That is finally more than the black elf is willing to bear. The maligned suitor loses his shit.

Alberich's blood is boiling. His groin is hot with burning desire. He wants these damn girls, and is determined to catch at least one of them and drag her down with him. But his threatening gestures are futile, because the watery ladies are faster than the awkward Nibelung, and even the shrimp laugh at the figure he cuts. The elf jumps from rock to rock, chasing the slithering maidens, trying to grab them. Resounding laughter is the answer. It's three graceful divers against one heavy-handed Gollum. And as the three Rhenish graces continue to taunt him, he curses loudly, panting and raging, shaking his fist at them.

The noise awakens something below, and the golden eye of the Rhine opens. The light on the water shimmers and gleams. What is it that glitters down there in the cool riverbed, what is the source of this resplendence the Rhine daughters bathe in? Why, that is the sacred Rhinegold. Alberich feels an irresistible lure, and asks the beauties what this underwater brilliance is. Wellgunde is naïve enough to tell him about the magical powers of the Rhinegold. This submerged treasure holds the secret to ruling the world. She tells him that the man who forges a ring from the Rhinegold will gain unlimited power, and thus become Lord of the entire world.

Flosshilde reminds the sisters of their father's order, which was to guard the treasure so that nobody would take it. Wellgunde and Woglinde however are rather arrogant in their certainty that the gold is safe, reminding their sister of the conditions for gaining its powers: *Only he who forswears love's power, only he who forfeits love's delight, only he can attain the magic to fashion the gold into a ring.* In other words: If you want to be Lord of the Ring, you need to forsake love for now and forever. That is the Rhinegold's secret.

And who in their right mind, the sisters argue, would relinquish love for all eternity, just to gain the power invested in the gold? Surely not a wretch such as Alberich, who was squirming with love's ardor just a few moments earlier! The Rhine ladies are convinced that everything that lives and breathes also dreams of love: No living thing would ever willingly abstain from love, and thus a guy like Alberich could never be a threat to the sunken treasure.

The taunted Nibelung overhears all that, and recognizes the fathomless value of the gold immediately. He ponders his options with a cool head. His logic is born from countless disappointments, long devoid of the hope for true love and real affection. Alberich concludes: If he can't force anyone to love him, at least he will be able to buy himself lust once he has forged the ring from the gold. This realization hits him like a flash of lightning, and *poof*, the first agent in this heroic drama has succumbed to the allure of the precious metal.

Alberich makes a momentous decision. He jumps into the churning waters of the Rhine and seizes the gold from the river, whose bright gleaming had always illuminated the girls' bathing hours. The sinister demon loudly forswears the joys of love forever: *I will put out your light, wrench the gold from the rock, forge the ring of revenge; for hear me, ye waves: thus I curse love!* Yes, the elf actually curses love itself. He subjects himself to the bewitching luster of the gold, intending to subdue the world, and to pay for the satisfaction of his lust.

The Rhine daughters are desperate. Alberich has stolen the Rhinegold from them. They have failed as its guardians. Who can help them now? They whine and lament, calling out in a many-voiced plea for help. Meanwhile, the confounded thief disappears into the dark depths of his lightless lair. The waters churn; the Rhine foams and fumes. Alberich's jeering laughter can be heard from far below. He has taken revenge on those who taunted him. He now possesses the magical gold and is ready to forge the One Ring. World domination is within his grasp—what more can he want? The sad and ghastly motif of the renunciation of love echoes and slowly ebbs away.

They say money corrupts, or money is the root of all evil. Both claims are debatable. Poverty does not save people from corruption, and even moderate wealth does not necessarily build character. But maybe those who were corrupt from the beginning can sink even lower when in the thrall of riches? Oh yes, they sure can!

The fuss over the legendary Rhinegold will prove that gold, and the power inherent in it, are the bearers of doom. The precious metal exerts an irresistible pull, a glamour that is also the curse that will be the downfall of humankind. That is the crucial message the drama of the ring of the Nibelung offers.

Gamblers on the Mountain of the Gods
(SCENE TWO)

The sound of horns heralds the dawn of a new day. While the robber from Nibelheim is stacking the stolen gold in his cave down there in the Rhine valley, a pair of gods is still sleeping soundly on a flower-carpeted mountain plateau, high above the river. It's Wotan and his wife Fricka, resting in spite of what has transpired below. Theirs is the sleep of the just—for what do the gods care about the misery of some nymphs of mean birth? The morning arrives, the mists clear, and on a mountaintop on the other side of the river, a proud stronghold shines brightly in the light of the rising sun.

Fricka wakes up and stretches, her eyes fall on the castle. She is impressed, and quickly shakes the boss awake from his dreams of power and wealth: *Wotan, husband, awake!* He stirs, opens his eye, and is captivated by the sight as well. The stronghold of the gods that he commissioned has been completed! He sees the magnificent building in broad daylight for the very first time. Finally the castle, which he has seen in his dreams a hundred times, is finished. This is the folly of the gods; a structure Wotan had rhapsodized about, satisfying his desire to project his power and greatness. Now it has become reality, and is awaiting its new inhabitants.

Richard Wagner composed themes, or motifs, for each event and every character, and here it is time for the Walhall motif. This technique of repetition was the latest modern invention in music, which Wagner had plagiarized from Berlioz. While the Frenchman called it leitmotif, Wagner rechristened it *remembrance motif*.

Wotan rejoices, but Fricka is anxious, for she knows that with the completion of the castle, the agreed payment is due as well. In order to fulfill his dream of a residence befitting his rank and status, Wotan had offered his wife's younger sister as compensation to the builders, two giants that went by the names of Fasolt and Fafner. His sister-in-law Freia was not only a pretty creature and the caretaker of the divine gardens, now she was also the token promised the master builders for the creation of the glorious mansion.

With this payment in kind, the boss of the godly crew had intended to get the owners of Fasolt & Fafner, Inc. to do their best and produce a masterpiece for him. But Wotan is a cheat. He plans to deprive them of their expected reward, hoping to fob them off in a different currency. For this plan, he enlisted his adjutant, the cunning Loge, who promised him a clever solution to the dilemma. The demigod has already handled a number of shady business deals between heaven and earth for Wotan.

So when Fricka berates her husband now, he remains calm and unfazed. *Reckless man, recall the price to be paid.* Her husband waves it away, telling her not to worry about that small payment issue. But Fricka won't be silenced. She reminds him how the men negotiated the building contract without consulting the women, resulting in the bartering away of her own sister. *What do you harsh men hold sacred and valuable when you thirst for power?* Wotan counters by reminding his wife that she was the one who desired a sizable residence.

The discussion about the castle reveals a lot about the private lives of the divine couple. Fricka wants to bind Wotan to her side—like a female bird taking possession of her nest. She wants to dazzle and ensnare Wotan with that pompous home and its opulent furnishings, so he stops roaming and casting his eye on other women, because her better half is all to prone to that: *All who live love roaming and variety; I cannot relinquish this sport.* Alas, he loves women too much, at least in Fricka's opinion, though to be fair, he once gave one of his eyes in a fight for her. And he says he has no intention of giving up Freia either.

On that cue, sister-in-law Freia comes running, looking for help. The giant Fasolt, one of the two master builders, has just let her know that he is coming for her. Wotan places his bets on Loge and his wiles, because: *When he counseled this contract, he promised to deliver Freia: on him I now rely.* But Loge is nowhere in sight, and the sound of the stomping approach of the giants is unmistakable. Desperate, Freia calls out to her divine brothers, Donner and Froh.

And then the brawny builders show up, carrying heavy clubs. Their entry is accompanied by a hefty musical motif involving kettledrums, bass and contrabass tubes, and other brass instruments. Fasolt and Fafner erected the mighty castle while the gods were sleeping soundly. By the sweat of their brows they moved and stacked heavy stones to create the magnificent mansion that Fasolt now points out to his client, singing in his giant's bass: *There stands what we raised, brightly shining in the light of day: now pass in and pay us our fee!*

Wotan acts the part of the generous owner and asks the workers how much they want, even though he knows the answer full well. Fasolt acts as the spokesman of the heavy laborers, reminding him of their contract and of Freia, whom they want to carry off home as their reward. Quickly, Wotan objects and even goes so far as to insult the giants. He asks them whether they are out of their minds with their so-called contract, and tells them to come up with another price, because Freia is not available.

The giants can hardly believe their ears: Wotan betrays the contract he sealed with his spear! The father of the gods turns out to be a cheat, no better than a common card shark. The pair gets very angry, but Fasolt restrains himself and tries one more time to settle this amicably. He reminds Wotan of the fact that his power as chief of the gods rests solely on contracts, and that peaceful coexistence can only be guaranteed if all parties honor their agreements.

Wotan goes all out with his rhetoric, trying to dismiss the deal as a joke. And again, he is careless enough to insult the hard-working giants: *The lovely goddess, bright and light, of what use is her charm to you louts?* Now the "louts" have had enough and really work up steam: *We dullards toil away, sweating, with our horny hands, to win a woman who, winsome and gentle, will live with us poor creatures: and do you now upset our bargain?*

Fafner tells his brother to shut up and grab the girl. He knows that Freia's job is to take care of the apples in the divine orchard. The golden apples from her garden are the source of the gods' eternal youth, so without her husbandry, their star will wane quickly. If they want to maintain their immortality, Freia is indispensable.

The giants are done with negotiating; they demand Wotan's decision. He refuses to honor their deal, so they grab Freia, but then her brothers Donner and Froh come barging in. A giant brawl seems imminent. The belligerent god of thunder wants to hit them with his heavy hammer, but they remain calm, claiming that they have come to receive their promised pay, and that they don't want to start a war. But the altercation escalates, and the parties yell at each other, until Wotan steps between them with his spear. The shaft of his weapon is said to protect and vouchsafe contracts. A moment of truce.

Then finally Loge appears. Wotan hopes that his friend will deliver a solution to his delicate dilemma. But Loge disappoints him by praising the reliable work of the giants. They created the castle exactly the way the divine family commissioned it. Wotan does not want to hear any of it. He presses Loge to come up with one of his cunning ideas, to suggest a more valuable substitute for Freia. The giants growl impatiently: they want their due now!

Loge reports that he went to all four corners of the world to look for an adequate replacement for Freia, but that his search was in vain. He now knows that *nothing is so rich than a man will accept it in lieu of woman's beauty and delight.* On his quest he saw only one man who had forsworn love: *For shining gold he had renounced woman's affection.* That man was Alberich, the night elf, the man who stole the Rhinegold. The Rhine daughters by the way were entreating Wotan to help them, to save the treasure and return it to the waters where it belonged.

Wotan does not care. He has his own predicament to deal with; he can't be bothered with helping anyone else right now. Meanwhile the giants process what they overheard: They are familiar with the Nibelung; he has caused them trouble before, but always managed to get away with it. If he has all that gold in his possession now, they expect new attacks and shenanigans from him. They ask Loge how much the treasure is worth, and he reveals its secret to all those present: If the hoard is forged into a ring, the ring bearer becomes ruler of the world!

That makes Fricka's ears perk up, for she dreams of beautiful jewelry, and wants to secure Wotan's faithfulness with dazzling adornment. But Loge tells the gods that they are too late. Alberich has already renounced love and proceeded to forge the mighty magic ring. By the power of the ring, the midget will soon be able to subjugate both gods and giants.

Wotan immediately proclaims greedily: *I must have the ring!* As father of the gods, Wotan is lord of the world after all, and needs to defend this claim any way he can. The forged product no longer requires forswearing love either, and Loge suggests that it will be easy to attain: *By theft! What a thief stole, you steal from the thief: could possessions be more easily acquired?*

Fasolt and Fafner are fascinated with Loge's tale, too. He seems to have told them all this without any hidden agenda, but bear in mind, this is the wily One. The giants begrudge the black elf his gold, and they even think it is worth more than Freia. If they had the magic ring, they could win their own immortality by simple coercion. Thus Fafner steps forward and tells Wotan their decision: *Freia may stay with you in peace; an easier fee I've found in settlement: we rough giants would be satisfied with the Niblung's shining gold.*

Wotan starts fuming once again. Are the giants insane? They want him to give them what he does not have? Shall he catch the elf for the benefit of some dumb behemoths? He calls them shameless and excessive in their demand.

The two giants are fed up with their faithless client and his insults. They simply grab the original reward and stomp off with their giant steps—across the Rhine, back to Riesenheim. Freia, goddess of youth and guardian of the golden apples, is in their power. If Wotan wants to have his pretty sister-in-law back, he needs to bring them the Rhinegold by the end of the day.

You don't have to be a horticulturist to be interested in the fact that the oft-quoted golden apples were probably actually oranges, originally called apples from China. Even in antiquity, citrus plants already played a prominent role: Think of the legendary "golden apples" that grew in the garden of the Hesperides, the daughters of the night. These oranges were guarded by the dragon-headed serpent Ladon, which never slept. The Olympian Heracles was sent by king Eurystheus of Mycenae to steal the precious apples. The hero slew the guardian animal and brought home the fruit, thus solving one of his twelve "Herculean tasks."

Wotan and his fellow gods strike up their lamentation accordingly. Loge, who had rarely ever been allowed to take a bite of the apples of immortality, being only a demigod and all, finds it amusing how quickly the ageing process catches up with the mighty gods: The heavy hammer slips from Donner's grip. Froh looks tired, and Wotan's beard turns iron gray. They didn't have their breakfast of fruit yet, and now the gardener is a pawn in the hands of the giants. Soon the apples are going to decay and fall to the ground, rotten and spoiled. And without those apples, the family tree of the gods is going to wither, grow old and gray, geriatric and bowed down with grief, the wilting object of the world's derision.

Again it is Fricka who pesters her husband and decries his foolishness. Wotan has had enough. He is a man of action, and as such orders Loge to descend into Nibelheim with him to win the stolen gold. Loge reminds him of the Rhine daughters, who hope for help from the father of the gods. But Wotan cares only about his deal with the giants, and about getting Freia and her apples back. The divine tribe needs the regenerating fruit, the golden apples of youth from her orchard. Wotan is willing to turn into a thief to reach his aim.

He is not willing however to take the road through the river Rhine, because he knows the Rhine daughters are waiting for his help down there, and he does not want to have to deal with them. The only other passage to Nibelheim leads through a sulfurous cleft in the mountain, ripe with poisonous vapors and awful smells. But Wotan and Loge brave the disagreeable path, for they don't have a choice.

The Nibelheim Heist
(SCENE THREE)

The descent into the sulfurous cleft is reminiscent of a trip into hell, or a journey to the center of the earth. The sound of hammering reveals what busy smiths the subterranean dwellers are. Deep down below the surface, they work without pause, for the dwarves are famed goldsmiths. The uninviting Nibelheim is anything but a peaceful workshop however; hammering, forging and filing are not the only things going on there: Alberich, the absolutist ruler over all the other small people, is in the process of torturing his brother Mime, who is known as an especially skillful blacksmith. His clever brother wants him to forge a magic helmet from the Rhinegold, an item that would enable him to shift into any desired form, or to become invisible.

But Mime is a devious one as well. He wants to keep the precious helmet for himself, and make use of the magic it contains. Alberich reacts without warning, seizing the artfully wrought piece from the artistic blacksmith and putting it on his own head. The magic works, and Alberich becomes invisible. He beats up his brother for the attempt to steal from him. He doesn't let up until Mime lies in the corner, crying and groaning.

Clad in his new magic garment, Alberich feels almighty. He possesses the ring of power, which he forged from the Rhinegold, and now he also possesses the ability to become invisible or morph into whatever he wants. He will be able to control and spy on his Nibelung nation without them even noticing him. They are doomed to eternal drudgery, forced to dig for gold in each tiny cleft and crack that Alberich finds with the help of the ring's powers. Jubilant, he hurries off to try out his new magic on his minions. The Nibelungs' many-voiced lamentation can be heard from the background, where the invisible tyrant whips them to work harder.

Wotan and Loge listen to the wails, and then Loge approaches Mime, who is related to him as a cousin, and offers his help. The dwarf doesn't think that someone from outside can release him, for it was his own brother who shackled him. Loge is surprised, asking how that was possible at all: *But what, Mime, gave him the power to bind you?* The blacksmith tells him how Alberich forged a yellow ring from the Rhinegold, whose powerful spell they all must succumb to. The Nibelung used to be a society of carefree dwarves, who made cute little baubles for their wives, but the black elf turned them into an army of slaves, who are forced to accumulate more and more wealth for their master.

Mime also tells them about the magic helmet, which he forged for Alberich without grasping its secret. Now that Alberich has revealed what the helmet can do, the welts on his abused back remind him of his stupidity. He has lost all hope to ever escape the drudgery that his own brother has subjected him to—he knows he is to remain a slave for all eternity. He barely manages to warn the wanderers of the dark demon, before Alberich returns. He yells and drives a horde of Nibelung in front of him with his whip. They must stack silver and gold jewelry to form a huge pile, a hoard. Then he notices the uninvited guests and feels disturbed by their intrusion.

He orders all his Nibelung including Mime to get back to work, prospecting for more gold. He cows them by pulling the heavy gold ring from his finger and pointing it at them: *Tremble with terror, abject throng: at once obey the master of the ring!* The Nibelung howl with fear and disperse, slipping into the holes and shafts below. Wotan and Loge have now witnessed the power of the magic ring firsthand, and Wotan's greed is rekindled anew. He wants both the ring and the rest of the hoard, in order to ransom Freia from the giants. But how can they seize the treasure from Alberich?

Wotan starts flattering Alberich, and tells him of the legendary reputation Nibelheim enjoys, thanks to his miraculous feats. He claims that they came to see whether the tales about him and his fabulous wealth were true. The ruler of the dwarves suspects they might be drawn by envy alone, and thus remains wary. But he can't help bragging and displaying his continuously growing pile of riches to his cousin Loge, who wants to know the use of such a hoard in a joyless place such as Nibelheim, where you cannot even spend any of the gold.

Alberich has his own ideas about what to do with his wealth. He wants to work wonders and subjugate the world. First of all, he wants to turn all the gods into money-grubbing maniacs, and then proceed to force their pretty women to satisfy his lust, all those who scorned him before. His revenge is the lure of riches; he wants money to make the world go round.

It is time for Loge to take over: He praises Alberich's plan, and prophesies that even the sun, moon and stars must serve the mighty gnome in the end. But he advises him to keep his Nibelung in check, for while they tremble before the ring now, what might happen if one of them steals it while Alberich is asleep? Alberich laughs it off, and calls out his demigod cousin for thinking everyone else is stupid enough to fall for his tricks. He says that he is protected by a magic helmet his brother Mime made, which enables him to shift into anything he wants. *No one can see me, though he search for me; yet I am everywhere, hidden from sight. Thus I can live carefree, safe even from you, kind, considerate friend!*

Loge seems duly impressed. Never before has he witnessed such magic, making it hard to believe that it is truly possible. But if Alberich spoke the truth, his power would last forever, he quips. The demigod appeals to his cousin's honor: He wants to see the helmet's powers with his own eyes; otherwise he won't believe it exists. Alberich fumes and says, fine, so in what form do you want to see me? And Loge answers: *In whatever you will: strike me dumb with astonishment!*

Alberich puts the helmet on his head, and then his mighty bass resounds: „*Giant snake, curl and coil!*" He shapeshifts into a Tatzelwurm, which is basically a giant serpent or dragon without wings, and snatches at the visitors. Loge acts as if he were whining and begging for his life, while Wotan jests about the speed with which the puny dwarf has turned into a huge dragon.

The Tatzelwurm disappears, and Alberich is back in his normal form. *Hehe! Clever ones, do you belive me now?* Loge professes to be deeply impressed by this metamorphosis into something so large and terrifying; in fact, he is still trembling from the experience. But he still has another question: Is the mighty Alberich able to turn himself into something small as well, or is that too hard? Alberich accepts the challenge with disdain: *Too hard for you because you're stupid! How small shall I be?* Loge answers: *So that the narrowest crevice might hold you, where a toad timidly hides.*

Pah, that's a walk in the park for Alberich. He puts the helmet back on his head, mutters another spell, and poof, there is an ugly toad on the ground. Loge immediately tells Wotan to seize the animal, and the older god puts his foot down on it. Loge reaches for its head and grabs the invisible helmet, and Alberich shifts back into his normal form again.

The Nibelung squirms under Wotan's foot, and despite his strenuous opposition, he is bound hand and feet by his cousin Loge. The two intruders carry their captive back to the sulfurous cleft, and hasten to climb back up to the surface with their prey.

Alberich, robber of the Rhinegold, has fallen victim to robbers himself.

The Curse of the Ring
(SCENE FOUR)

Wotan has clearly won the last round. Alberich, the thief of the Rhinegold, bearer of the magic helmet, and lord of the ring of power, is his prisoner now, thanks to Loge's cunning. Now the two drag their captive back out of Nibelheim and up the mountain, to the plateau where the gods reside.

Once they arrive, Loge performs a little victory dance and taunts the prisoner. Alberich gets angry and threatens terrible revenge if they don't take off the fetters immediately. He had thought the world was already his for the taking, and now this iniquity! If he wants to exact revenge, he first needs to come up with a hefty ransom, as Loge makes clear.

The dwarf wants to know how much his captors demand. Wotan's answer comes quickly: *The treasure and your gleaming gold*. Alberich rants and raves, calling the kidnappers a "*greedy gang of rogues*." He secretly hopes that he will be able to keep the ring, because with the power invested in that trinket alone, he could always assemble a new hoard. The wealth he has so far accumulated seems an appropriate premium for his own stupidity, so he agrees to the demanded ransom. Wotan frees one of his hands so he can call his minions. The black elf kisses the ring and mutters an order, and soon enough, his servants crawl from the cleft, carrying the jewelry from the hoard.

Alberich is ashamed to be seen by his minions in shackles. Therefore he tells them to make haste and return to Nibelheim. A giant heap of gold and silver has been brought before Wotan and Loge. Alberich hopes to get away so easily: *I have paid: now let me depart.* He asks Loge to give back the helmet, but his cousin throws it on top of the hoard and says that this trophy is part of the ransom.

The Nibelung curses the thief loudly, but secretly tells himself to remain calm. Because as long as he still possesses the ring, he can simply order his brother Mime to forge him a new helmet. The main thing now is to regain his freedom. He demands of Wotan and Loge: *Alberich has left you everything: now, bullies, loosen my bonds!*

But Wotan knows exactly what he wants. He asks for the golden ring on Alberich's finger, claiming that it is part of the treasure, and therefore part of the ransom. The Nibelung trembles: *My life, but not the ring!* Wotan remains impassive: *I require the ring: with your life do what you will!*

Alberich writhes and whines, because that ring is the only thing left of his fabled riches. Wotan barks at the elf that the ring is derived from the gold which he stole from the Rhine daughters, and the elf barks right back. He sees clearly that Wotan accuses him of a deed that he would gladly have done himself, had he known how to forge the ring. He goes on to make clear that while he only sinned against himself with his vow to renounce love, Wotan is about to sin against everything that ever was, is, and will be. Does he really want to seize the ring?

The god doesn't want to listen to another word, for he probably senses the truth in what the dwarf said. He grabs the Nibelung and pulls the ring from his finger, only to put it on his own. The imperious god has reached his goal: *Now I possess what will make me the mightiest of mighty lords!*

Alberich breaks down crying, a mere shadow of his former self. He is unbound and told to get lost. But Wotan underestimates the dwarf. The defeated lord of the Nibelung stands straight and curses on the golden ring. Acquired through a curse, he now invests it with a new curse: *Since its gold gave me measureless might, now may its magic bring death to whoever wears it! It shall gladden no happy man; its bright gleam shall light on no one lucky! Whoever possesses it shall be consumed with care, and whoever has it not be gnawed with envy! Each shall itch to possess it, but none in it shall find pleasure!* And that is not all. He adds in a threatening voice: *Forfeit to death, faint with fear shall he be fettered; the length of his life he shall long to die, the ring's master to the ring a slave, until again I hold in my hands what was stolen!* That is the desperate blessing he bestows on his ring, before vanishing in the cleft.

Wotan has been far too engrossed in looking at his booty to listen closely to Alberich's words. Let the gnome rant, Wotan has achieved everything he had dreamed of. The raid on the Nibelung lair was successful. The ring is on his finger now, and the hoard is his to ransom Freia and pay off the giants. The new castle is finally paid for. Donner, Froh, and Fricka appear, and welcome the pilgrims home. They are happy to see that everything is ready to get the guarantor of eternal youth back. And on that cue, Fasolt and Fafner come stomping up the hill with their hostage.

Wotan greets the master builders and shows them the hoard. Fasolt demands that the gold be stacked around Freia, until she is no longer to be seen underneath the treasure. He has a harder time giving up the fair maiden than his brother Fafner. Thus he wants to gold to cover her so he can start to forget her. Out of sight, out of mind –Loge and Froh follow the motto and start stacking the gold around the goddess, until she is fully covered.

Fafner checks on the result, and can still see her shimmering hair. He turns to Loge, who is still holding the helmet, demanding that he throw it on top of the pile. Loge refuses, but Wotan orders him to relinquish the magic item. Now Freia seems to be hidden underneath the gold completely. It's Fasolt's time to check, and wouldn't you know it, her eye still beams at him from a crack in the stack. Fafner urges the gods to fill that last crack, but Loge berates the insatiable giants and tells them that no more gold is left. Fafner objects, because he has seen the gold ring that gleams on Wotan's finger. The gods shall yield the ring to fill the last gap in the mountain of gold.

Wotan refuses, angry and thoughtful. Loge tries to tell the giants that the ring belongs to the Rhine daughters, and that Wotan intends to return it to them. But the father of the gods does not play along: *What idle chatter is this? What I won with such difficulty without a qualm I'll keep for myself.* Loge gave the three maidens his promise, but Wotan does not feel bound to this oath. He wants to keep the ring for himself. The giants have enough of his stalling and trickery however. Fasolt pulls Freia out from behind the golden wall, proclaiming the exchange failed. Things will remain as they were, and Freia will continue to live in Riesenheim.

Fricka, Donner and Froh are stunned. They urge Wotan to give up the ring so the deal can still be brought to a happy ending. But Wotan refuses. He is adamant about keeping the ring of the Nibelung. Just then the earth opens up, and Earth Mother Erda rises from the realm of the dead, Hel. In her function as seer, she warns: *Yield, Wotan, yield! Escape from the ring's curse. To dark destruction irredeemably its possession dooms you.* Wotan has no idea who she is, until she reveals herself to be the *first ancestress*, and mother off the three Rhine daughters. He normally only speaks with Erda through the medium of the three Norns Urd (past), Werrdandi (present) and Skuld (future), who spin the thread of time at the wellspring of fate, located at the base of the ash tree that is the world, Yggdrasil.

But Erda has a good reason for appearing in person at this time, because suddenly everything that is, is in danger of ending. The imminent threat is the twilight of the gods, or the end of the world as we know it, and therefore Wotan should shun the cursed ring at all costs. She tells him to consider her warning in fear and dread. She sinks back into the earth, which closes over her again. Wotan wants to go after her, needs to know more, but Fricka and Froh stop the madman.

Donner asks the giants to wait; the gold will be given to them in full. Wotan still looks as if he's raving mad, but he slowly comes to. He grabs his spear and finally throws the ring onto the pile of gold, though it may be the hardest thing he's ever done. The treasure of the Nibelung belongs to the giants now. The payment is complete, and Freia is free again.

While the gods rejoice over the goddess' salvation, the giants start fighting over their booty. Fafner puts most of the gold into a humongous sack and leaves Fasolt to contend himself with the smaller share. After all, he had wanted Freia to himself, not willing to share her with his brother either. Fasolt invokes the gods to be the judge of this new trick, but they turn away in disdain. Loge is the only one who answers at all, advising him to take the ring instead of the hoard.

Fasolt lunges at Fafner, claiming the ring as a substitute for Freia's gaze. But Fafner grabs for the piece, too. They start wrestling for it, and then Fasolt seizes the ring from his older brother. Fafner takes his club and beats the younger one over the head. Fasolt falls to the ground, dead. Fafner takes the ring from his dying fingers and calmly collects the rest of the gold lying about. Stunned, the gods watch the spectacle of greed, and Wotan realizes that the terrible curse that Alberich bestowed upon the ring has just claimed its first victim.

Loge tries to comfort him, claiming that their enemies' killing each other because of the treasure is really a good thing. But Wotan is more concerned with the possibility of warding off the prophesied twilight of the gods. He wants to go down to where Erda lives, and ask her for advice. But Fricka is not happy with the prospect of her husband's visit with Erda, for he fathered several children on her in the past. In her jealousy she soft-soaps him into focusing on the wondrous new castle that awaits them in the mists over the Rhine.

The air is sultry with an impending thunderstorm. Donner swings his hammer, pulls the dark clouds together, and discharges them in a mighty flash of lightning. A brightly gleaming rainbow curves out from the mountain plateau, across the river and out to the splendid new digs. Wotan and the rest of the gods are speechless at the sight of the mighty fortress the giants erected for them. Wotan names their new castle Walhall. He takes Fricka's hand and leads her across the rainbow bridge to their new dwelling place. The other gods follow.

From the depths of the river below, the lament of the Rhine daughters echoes up. The maidens entreat them to return the Rhinegold, but Wotan orders Loge to make the nymphs shut up. The light elf taunts Wellgunde, Flosshilde and Woglinde, they should be content to bathe in the brilliance of the new castle. But the girls continue to sob and cry below, denouncing him as deceitful and cowardly, while he merely sneers at them.

The gods ignore the wronged maidens, stepping across their rainbow bridge towards Walhall, moving into the castle that will protect and defend them, and also reinforce their status. A massive surge of horns accompanies their march into Walhall.

Far, far below, the bereft Rhine daughters cry. Fafner, the fratricide, drags home the hoard, helmet and ring, bound for Riesenheim. Alberich, lord of the Nibelung, robber of the Rhinegold and forger of the ring, is not content with his curse; he wants revenge. And the all-knowing Earth Mother Erda sees the coming breakdown of the current world order.

THE VALKYRIE

First day of the scenic festival *The Ring of the Nibelung*

First performance: Munich,
Königliches Hof- und Nationaltheater
June 26, 1870

Characters in "The Valkyrie"

Siegmund, Wotan's son begotten from a human woman, is meant to recapture the ring

Sieglinde, Siegmund's twin sister, wife of Hunding

Hunding, a coarse huntsman who lives in a tree house in the woods

Wotan, boss of the god squad and unscrupulous potentate, tries to hold the reins both in heaven and on earth

Fricka, Wotan's wife and actual ruler of the pantheon, goddess of marriage and morals, wants to keep her husband in check and keep him from straying

Brünnhilde, Wotan's daughter begotten with the seer Erda, and his favorite Valkyrie

The Valkyries: Brünnhilde and her sisters Gerhilde, Ortlinde, Waltraute, Schwertleite, Helmwige, Siegrune, Grimgerde, Rossweisse, collect fallen warriors on the battlefields and bring them to Walhall to form a defense army.

ACT ONE

Manhunt in the Forest
(PRELUDE)

The orchestra opens the second part of *The Ring of the Nibelung* with a blustering, rising and falling prelude, a crescendo and diminuendo in D minor. It's the string section's turn: 32 violins, 12 violas, 12 violoncellos, and 8 contrabasses come together to describe a dramatic scene. A brutally determined gang of murderers is on a wild manhunt. The elements are in uproar.

The night is icy cold, the woods are pitch-black. A single man hastens through the seemingly boundless forest. He runs as fast as he can in the dark, becomes entangled in cobwebs, stumbles over roots and rotting logs. Torn and tattered garments are stuck to his frame, and he is injured, bleeding from numerous wounds. The exhaustion threatens to overwhelm him—he puffs and pants, sweats profusely. He throws a glance over his shoulder and stumbles onward. All the demons of hell seem to be on his track, breathing down his neck. He runs from death itself. His life is no longer worth a straw, because he's unarmed.

Horns are blown, signaling the angry hunters' determination to finally encircle him, finish this man with a drive hunt. They in turn are driven by blood vengeance. They communicate in hoarse shouts and crude commands. They can smell the cold sweat of their human prey as they follow his bloody trail. Steam rises from their horses' flanks. Soon the hunters will close the deadly circle around their victim. They will stab him, impale him, hack him to pieces and drink his blood. They will carry home his severed head as a trophy. Bloodlust drives the headhunters as they tear through the underbrush.

Overhead, lightning cracks and thunder rolls. A heavy rain pours down from the heavens, and the old branches groan. In Walhall, the gods are sitting in front of their surveillance monitors, watching the drama down below. Wotan, father of the gods, finally lifts a protective hand and gives the lost soul on the run a reprieve. He has plans for the hunted man, great plans. And suddenly the distance between the runner and his pursuers grows. A drawn-out drum roll announces a turn in the manhunt. The bloodhounds, confident of their victory only a moment ago, lose track of their prey. Their angry howls echo through the forest. Is this the hunted man's salvation?

The refugee crawls forward on all fours now, dragging himself into a wide clearing in the heart of the forest. A giant Ash tree towers before him, its branches far up in the sky. On the side of the shimmering trunk of the world tree, a sturdy timber house sits in its shade. The mighty broadleaf has grown through the roof of the cottage, spreading its leaves over it in protection. Smoke rises from the house's chimney, and the air smells of aromatic charcoal. Flickering light seeps from the hatches. The hunted man stumbles towards the house, opens the groaning door with his last reserve of strength, drags himself over to the glowing stove, and sinks down in front of it. He does not care anymore, for he cannot go on. His fate is in the hands of the gods. The orchestra falls silent.

In the Enemy's House
(SCENE ONE)

Whoever's fire place this may be, here I must rest. These are the final words of the hunted man before he breaks down on the floor of the cottage he has invaded. The mistress of the house hears a noise and thinks that her husband has come home from hunting. When she sees the stranger instead, she is startled, but addresses him anyway. He doesn't react, doesn't stir at all. She approaches warily and realizes that he is weakened, but alive.

Then suddenly the man wakes up with a jolt. He half-rises and begs for water. She grabs a drinking horn and runs out, to the nearby spring, where she fills the horn and offers it to the blood-spattered intruder. He greedily drains the horn in one big gulp, and immediately, his spirits are revived. He offers her a grateful smile and wants to know where he is, and who his helpful hostess may be.

She tells him that this is Hunding's house, and that she is Hunding's wife. She offers him hospitality in her husband's name and says that he will be home soon, too. The hunted man rises and shows her that he is unarmed and injured: *A wounded guest will not worry your husband.* He tells her that he was hounded by enemies and that his weapons broke. He ran from the bloodthirsty pack, and ended up in a thunderstorm that put him over the edge.

His hostess fills the horn again, but this time she offers him mead. He asks her to take the first sip, before gulping down the sweat drink. Thus fortified, he is ready to take his leave again. He says he merely needed a brief rest, and doesn't want to cause trouble for her. He confesses that whichever way he turns, bad luck follows in his footsteps, and therefore he wants to leave quickly, lest he rewards her mercy with calamity.

He gets as far as the door, before she asks him to stay. Bitterly, she exclaims: *You cannot bring bad luck into the house where bad luck lives.* The refugee is shocked by the sudden frankness of this stranger, who bares her soul to him. Their misery draws them together. When he searches her face, their senses tell them that they "know" each other. And hence the guest decides to stay: *I named myself "Woeful". I will wait for Hunding.*

Hunding Appears
(SCENE TWO)

The pair at the hearth is startled by the sound of approaching hooves: The landlord is coming; Hunding arrives. Armed to the nines with shield and spear the hunter stomps into the cottage, immediately spying the unknown fellow who seems to have made himself comfortable in his absence. The orchestration underscores the sinewy entrance with a dire motif that spells threat. Brutality has stepped onto the stage.

In a show of anticipatory obedience, his wife explains: *I found this man exhausted, by our fireplace. Distress led him into our house.* In his deep bass, Hunding wants to know more: Did she offer anything to this dude? Yes, the wife did what a good hostess is meant to do, and took care of the refugee. The stranger asks his host whether he really wants to scold his wife for giving him shelter and drink.

The gruff landlord comes around. Of course he respects the right to hospitality. This Germanic custom is one of the basic social norms of its era. It protects the guest from eventual attacks by the host. This right to hospitality is inviolable, even for Hunding: *My hearth is holy. Treat my house as holy too.* He hands his weapons to his wife to put them away, and orders her to serve them dinner.

Hunding and his guest sit down at the heavy table next to the hearth. The landlord studies the stranger in the flickering light of the fire and finds his features strangely familiar. They're very much like those of his wife! They actually look like two peas in a pod. They share the same bold and unfettered gaze. Hunding hides his surprise, and asks where his foreign guest comes from. He cares about clan connections, houses, families and thus, names. What bad fortune led the injured man so deep into the forest? And without a horse, to boot! He must have come a long way on foot ...

The stranger relates how he traversed all manner of terrain, being hunted by storm and distress, until he lost his way completely. He has no idea where he is right now. Hunding introduces himself with great pride, claiming to be part of a clan that owns most of the estates to the West of his cottage. He is related to a lot of people who protect the honor of their common blood. But now he wants to know the name and origin of his guest.

Lady Hunding has taken a seat next to her husband and is staring at their guest. She is conspicuously interested in the mysterious visitor, obviously just as eager to know who he is. In a plaintive voice, the stranger says that he calls himself "Woeful" and explains why: His life is haunted by bad luck, and he has caused misery to many. When he was still a boy, he came home from hunting with his father, Wolf, to find their home desolate and empty. An enemy tribe of ruffians had burned down the wolf's lair. His mother lay slaughtered in the rubble, and his twin sister had been abducted. All they had left now was their bare lives.

Father and son fled into the woods and fought off their pursuers, who kept chasing and attacking them. At some point the boy was separated from his father, and all that remained of him was a wolf's coat. Since that day, he calls himself Woeful, the last surviving wolf-cub.

Hunding's scowl deepens during this tale. This father of his strange guest reminds him too much of the stories he's heard about the werewolf, who can shift from an animal to a human monster, leaving behind only his coat. The son of a werewolf means bad luck indeed. He's cursed by the Norns, the goddesses of fortune, and rightly so. He isn't happy to have such a guest under his roof.

His wife on the other hand hangs on the wolf-cub's lips, enrapt by his story. She wants to know more. How did he lose his weapons?

Now Woeful ramps it up with a wild ballad: He had offered his protection to a young woman that was to be married against her will. Chivalrous libertine that he is, he came to her aid and wanted to protect her honor. A fight ensued and he ended up slaughtering part of her clan, including her two brothers. Then the tribesmen arrived, out for vengeance. The angry attackers hacked his spear and shield to pieces, and the girl ended up stabbed to death. Injured and unarmed, he could barely get away with his life. His enemies hunted him through the forest, until the gods led him to Hunding's cottage.

The injured guest turns to Lady Hunding and finishes his story with the words: *Woman, you asked; now you know why I am not called „Peaceful".* She feels compassion and sympathy, for she was forced into a loveless marriage, too. A love match was more or less unheard-of in Germanic times. But the mysterious visitor does not seem to want to submit to the zeitgeist. But to give credit to the curmudgeonly Hunding, he took a wife that had been displaced in the turmoil of war (as the plot will reveal soon enough), even though she had no favorable clan background.

But now the owner of cottage and woman explodes with rage. He jumps up and points his finger at his wolven guest: He had been part of the posse that was called to avenge the spilled blood of his clansmen, but he arrived too late at the scene of the crime. So he went home empty-handed, only to find the culprit resting in his own abode. The only thing that protects *"the villain who fled"* now is the sacred right to hospitality. But the ruffian clansman wants his revenge. He challenges the wolf-cub to a fight at dawn. Then he orders his wife to retire to the bedroom, grabs his weapons, and demands that she make him a nightcap.

A breathless silence ensues. While Hunding stomps into his bedchamber and starts to plot his revenge, his wife and the wolf-cub exchange meaningful glances. She tries to direct his gaze to a specific spot on the trunk of the ash tree that is part of the house. Woodwinds, bass trumpet, oboe and English horn come together to play a motif that was introduced at the end of the "Rhinegold," namely: The sword motif. As is often the case, the music already knows more than the characters, hinting at connections and developments.

Meanwhile the wife fills a drinking horn with mead for her husband, spicing it up with a mysterious powder from the witches' kitchen of wise women. Then she follows her husband into the bedchamber, and they latch the door from the inside.

The mysterious wolf man lies down in front of the hearth, ruminating on his desperate situation. He has stepped straight into the lion's den, so to speak, and now he has only one night to think of a way of escaping. Not an easy feat for an injured, weakened, unarmed man—and in his case aggravated by the bad luck that Woeful attracts like a magnet.

Fateful One-Night Stand
(SCENE THREE)

Hunding has barricaded himself in his bedchamber, together with his wife and weapons, where he dreams the night away. His unwelcome guest is wide awake and brooding. If only he had a weapon ... His father once promised him that in the hour of greatest distress, he would find a sword ... Father, where is that damn blade now?

And just in this dire predicament, he meets a "*radiant woman*," "*lovely and dignified*," who captivates his heart and bewitches him with her sweet spell. Instead of conquering her heart like a hero, he must suffer the scorn of her possessor. What a shitty situation for an unconventional free-thinker! He vents his frustration in song, while the gods on duty at the celestial command center pull a few stops. They're very adept at this, causing a log to fall in the fireplace, while he is still belting out his woes. The embers scatter and illuminate that one spot on the trunk of the ash, the one that Lady Hunding had stared at so meaningfully before. The hilt of a sword is clearly visible in the glimmer for a moment, but the refugee thinks he is hallucinating: *Is it the Gaze of that radiant woman that she left there clinging behind her when she went out of the room?* The man has fallen in love, alas! And as we know, love is blind, so he does not see the saving sword.

Soon the fire dies down and he is plunged in total darkness. And soon after that, the door of the chamber is opened and the mistress slips out in her nightgown. She confides that she gave her husband a drugged drink, in order to show him both herself and the weapon that is reserved for the strongest man.

On her wedding day, a one-eyed old man in a blue robe appeared and thrust a sharp sword into the trunk of the tree—

all the way to its hilt. Many men have since tried to pull the sword out, but none of them could move it even a fraction of an inch. The story of the enchanted sword in the ash tree brought many a muscle man to their cottage, but even the strongest failed, and went away empty-handed.

But now she says she knows who is meant to have the magic sword: The man who avengers her disgrace and dishonor, the hero she promises to embrace in return. The weakened warrior doesn't need to be told twice; he grabs the lady. We don't know whether the Germanic right to hospitality included the use of the landlady, but the injured man is no stickler for the letter of the law. He takes what is offered, much like his father who taught him to never waste an opportunity. Woeful presses against her inviting chest, declaring that he is the one meant to have sword and sorceress.

Wotan, father of the gods, has already been sitting in the director's chair for a while now, and now he pulls another lever to expedite the inevitable: The front door opens up, and the silver light of the full moon bathes the imminent couple in its enchanting light. It must have been spring who sprung the door, and now laughs victoriously, because he has vanquished the storm and cold of winter. Divine music resounds.

What follows is not only one of the longest, and therefore most exhausting scenes that Wagner has woven into his *Ring*—it is also one of the musically most beautiful, most lyrical, most intense, and for the singer the most demanding moment, initiated by the strings.

The man at the hearth soars into an aria that demands all of his talent. Not only does he want to bewitch the woman at his side, he also needs to give it his all so the audience feels a pleasant shiver run down their spines. This requires a powerful tenor, who is able to describe this intimate moment in a gentle, but at the same time formidable manner. The orchestra is ablaze; six harps pluck their strings like there's no tomorrow.

Wintry storms have vanished before May-time. In his aria he describes how a personified Spring defeats Jack Frost, letting his mild, gentle winds breeze through forests and meadows. *Marvelous flowers sprout from its hot blood, buds and shoots grow from its strength.* Honi soit qui mal y pense. The suddenly revived minstrel is not merely talking of the birds and the bees. He goes on to argue that Spring also lures out the love that had hidden from view in the cold season. Spring and Love are actually siblings, and all the barriers between them have been blown away by his balmy breezes: *Joyfully the young couple greet one another. Love and Spring are united.*

This is an opera, so they don't get down to business that quickly. Another quarter hour is passed in passionate song, before the big bang happens. I recommend closing your eyes, giving yourself up to the music, because onstage, excellent singers are doing their best work in those fifteen minutes. Unfortunately however, many high-caliber singers tend to be conspicuously corpulent. While that may increase the resonating body, and thus the voice volume, it sometimes gets in the way of the audience's imagination: Will that massive man in the fur coat and that "prima ton-a" in her tent-like dress really get down to having passionate sex once their song is finished? On the other hand it must be stated that closing one's eyes and getting immersed in the music bear their own risk: This is also the point in the entire *Ring* tetralogy when a lot of people in the audience fall asleep. The nodding heads around you are ample proof for that. But let's get on with the libretto.

The landlady is captivated by his song of the merry month of May, and responds by professing that this is exactly the kind of spring her joyless heart has been pining for. Then the soprano spills the beans: The young man before her must be the one friend she needs in this frigid, barren space. So she throws herself into his arms. A clear case of love at first sight.

The warrior is speechless. He can merely sigh of sweetest joy and blessed woman, before she presses closer and stares into his eyes. He is entranced by the way her hair shimmers in the moonlight, and can't get enough of looking at her: "*Rapturously my eyes gloat on you*," he gushes. The German original is even more flowery in its alliteration.

The woman feels that there is something wondrous going on, for she is certain that she has seen this man before. When her beau confides that he, too, saw her in some wet dream of "*courtly love*," she thinks this is uncanny. Remembering her features mirrored in a lake, she tells him that she sees herself in his sweet face. And she thinks that she also heard his voice before, when she was still a child.

Looking into his eyes, she talks of the old man that appeared on her wedding day again. When he thrust the sword into the ash tree, she felt a familiarity that had almost caused her to call him "*father*." The resemblance is striking. Is her lover-to-be really called Woeful?

He confesses, no, he is called neither Woeful nor Peaceful, but she can name him anything she wants. Just to be sure, she pushes on: Didn't he call his father "*Wolf*" before? He blurts that his father had been Volsa, a man from the Volsung tribe.

Now she is all excited, and her singing speeds up so much that the strings have a hard time keeping up with it. If her suitor's father was a Volsung, then that's what the son is, too. For him, the sword was thrust into the tree; a weapon for victory. She will accordingly call him *Siegmund*, a name that includes the Germanic term for victory, "Sieg." Finally the hunted stranger that found shelter in his mortal enemy's house has a name: *Siegmund*!

Now the violinists down in the pit really put the pedal to the metal—or rather, put the bow to the strings, speeding up. The warrior stands proud, grabs the sword by its hilt und rejoices in his new name: *Siegmund I am called and Siegmund I am!* His father Volsa had prophesied that he would find a sword when he needed it most. And now that dire moment had arrived. He decides that the sword will be called "*Nothung*," which is supposed to mean "that which is needed" in this context. The orchestra gallops along. Effortlessly, he pulls the steel from the tree, swinging it around for everyone to see. And he sings with joy and determination: *Nothung, Nothung, precious blade, show your sharpness and cutting edge: come from your scabbard to me!*

The lady is delighted. Her suitor places the magic sword at her feet, as a bridal offering. He wants to escape with her from the enemy's house, into springtime's smiling home, where he intends to protect her with Nothung's help. Now it's her turn to tell him her name, because if he is Siegmund, then she is Sieglinde, the woman who has been waiting for him to arrive. And that is not all, for she is also his twin sister, kidnapped by enemies while he was out hunting with their father: "*Sieglinde*!"

There is no more holding back Siegmund. The tuba players in the pit go wild. The hero grabs the heroine and tears off her nightshirt: *Wife and sister you'll be to your brother. So let the Volsung blood increase.* The orchestra knows that what is about to happen may be the hottest one night stand in the history of opera, so they go all in—or all out, as the case may be. They summon up everything they have, while somewhere above, Wotan Volsa, the puppeteer who fathered the twins on one of his joyrides on earth with a mortal woman, is satisfied with his work. Things are going according to his plans. Love and spring have found each other. The music rises and swells, whips itself into a state of ecstasy. Siegmund and Sieglinde are all over each other, siring and begetting a new warrior. He will be the protagonist that Wotan needs for the thickening of the plot in the third part of the *Ring*: Siegfried, the free hero!

But we don't want to know any of that right now, because right now, the godfather quickly veils the actual act of love, switching off the full moon and dropping the curtain. With a mighty beat on the kettle drum, he also finishes the infernal music in the pit. The audience is left to imagine what exactly is going on behind the curtain.

To smooth everyone's feathers and cool down the heated atmosphere, the composer inserted a pause right there. The stagehands set up the backdrop for the second scene, while the musicians dampen their arousal with a cool sip of water. In the meantime, Siegmund and Sieglinde take care of producing the necessary offspring.

ACT TWO

A Marital Quarrel in Wallhall
(PRELUDE AND SCENE ONE)

The orchestra opens the second act of "The Valkyrie" with full steam. Fully armored and with a spear ready in his hand, Wotan, chief of the gods, is standing on a rock. He is content with what he orchestrated down below, and now he is waiting for his favorite daughter Brünnhilde, to give her further orders. Only a few beats later, she comes galloping in: up to her teeth in weapons, on a fiery steed, whooping out her war cries of: "*Hoyotoho!*"

Wotan tells her to hasten to the cabin in the woods, where his son Siegmund and Hunding will soon be fighting. Of course he thinks that the Volsung blood must be victorious, and therefore tells her to support Siegmund in the upcoming battle. Hunding is to be slaughtered and left at the site of the fight. Wotan does not want to welcome the man to Walhall, where the Valkyries normally bring the fallen warriors.

Brünnhilde is one of these Valkyries, actually the one who lent her name to this part of the "Ring." Let's focus on her for a moment, while she cries out joyfully and belligerently in her highest register: *Hoyotoho! Hoyotoho! Heiaha! Heiaha! Hoyotoho! Heiaha!* The soprano needs to belt it out up to the high c. This is the first appearance of the female protagonist of this "Ring" part, and she is called upon to act with high drama and great skill. The vocal demands are immense; no easy feat for any singer who attempts the part. A telling tidbit: Deborah Polaski, one of the celebrated interpreters of Brünnhilde, is dubbed "the animal" in opera circles …

In any case, the Valkyrie wants to get going ASAP, because she can already see Wotan's divine wife, Fricka, rush towards them in a chariot drawn by rams. From the relentless way the goddess is driving and whipping the cowering animals, Brünnhilde can see that her heavenly father is in for some serious marital trouble. She wants no part of this type of strife, however much she loves the other, warlike kind. Thus she yells out a few more "Hoyotoho!" and "Heiaha!" calls, before vanishing downstage.

Fricka comes barreling in on her sky chariot, and steps off in a huff. Wotan senses that this will be no idle chat, and merely groans: *The old storm, the old trouble! Yet I must make a stand.* The love he formerly felt for his matron has long grown cold. Their relationship has been reduced to a recurring and constant power struggle. You probably know the saying that behind every strong man, there is a strong woman. Fricka is a very strong woman, and she is the actual mistress (in the sense of mastery, not love) of the gods' realm. Wotan merely remains its figurehead.

Fricka explains that Hunding has appealed to her in her function as guardian of matrimony. He asked her *to punish the behavior of that impudent, blasphemous pair who have openly wronged a husband.* Wotan tries to placate her. The sounds of Siegmund's song of spring can be heard again when he tells her sanctimoniously that the power and magic of love are nothing evil, nothing that needs atonement.

Fricka gets even angrier. She loses her cool and appeals to the holiness of the marriage vows. But Wotan answers that a vow which binds people together who do not love each other is anything but holy. Fricka is stumped by this lapidary reply, but then she rants at him: The union of the twin couple Siegmung and Sieglinde is incest, plain and simple! *Marital intercourse between brother and sister! When did it ever happen that brother and sister were lovers?*

The insidious spring song melody comes up again, and Wotan gives her another casual answer: *Today you have seen it happen.* Things do happen spontaneously, even if they never happened before. And instead of being a judgmental bitch, Fricka should bless this union of love.

Nope. Fricka goes through the roof. She reminds her husband of the many times he cheated on her, always looking for opportunities to follow his horny instincts, always ridiculing her in the process. Reminds him, too, of how he broke her heart when he sired Brünnhilde, "*the bride of his desire,*" with the goddess Erda, and the other Valkyries, those "*uncouth girls,*" with other women. And to top it all off, his biggest sacrilege was siring the Volsung twins with some mundane human woman.

Wotan tries to justify his actions as some sort of divine plan for saving the world. He tells her that a special kind of hero is needed: a man who is free from the laws of the gods, and can thus accomplish that which the gods cannot.

His wife doesn't want to hear anything about his deceptively "deep thoughts." She asks what a mere man—guided by and dependent on the gods as he is—could achieve that the gods themselves are unable to achieve. After all, who breathed courage into men, "*Who lit up the fools' eyes?*" Fricka is fed up with being lied to. She demands that Wotan take away his protection from his incestuous offspring, that he take away the weapon he gave the Volsung: *Yes, the sword, the magical, strong, flashing sword that you, the god, gave to your son.*

Wotan won't have any of it. His secret plan involves Siegmund defeating Fafner with the help of the magical sword, and then taking back the ring of power. Wotan sired this son for the sole purpose of accomplishing this. That is why he thrust the steel into the ash tree; that is why he led Siegmund to Hunding's cabin to meet his twin sister and make love to her. But Fricka won't let him get away with it. Does her immortal husband want her to be the laughing stock of the gods; does he want to desecrate her so? Surely not!

Wotan feels cornered. He sees no way out but to concede that Fricka is right. He has clearly lost this round of their fight. But he still tries to slip the noose, summoning up all the rhetorical maneuvers of a seasoned politician. The goddess demands he let go of the Volsung boy—he promises. She warns him not to support him in the upcoming fight—and he promises he won't.

But Fricka isn't satisfied. She demands that Wotan look into her eyes and promise her to also call the Valkyrie Brünnhilde from Siegmund's side. The hard-pressed husband tries to trick her one last time: *The Valkyrie shall do as she pleases.* But the goddess knows her husband all too well. She also knows that the Valkyries are bound to their creator, and will always do his bidding. So she demands: *Forbid her to let Siegmund win.*

Wotan squirms like a worm at that. He says he cannot prevent an eventual Volsung victory, for after all the boy found the magical sword. Fricka shakes her head. If he can't take away the sword, he must invalidate it: *Then take away its magic, let it break in your serf's hands.* Siegmund is to meet Hunding unarmed and unprotected.

On that ominous cue, Brünnhilde comes a-galloping again with her usual cry of "*Hoyotoho!*" When Fricka spies the

Valkyrie that is supposed to take care of Siegmund, she demands a sacred oath from her husband: Brünnhilde must avenge Fricka's honor by destroying the Volsung.

Wotan, the big boss, is beaten. He takes the oath, crushed by her proud insistence. Head held high, Fricka gets back into her chariot and leaves, but not without snubbing Brünnhilde first: The military leader changed his plans, so the girl should go and receive her new orders. Yes, Fricka is the actual mistress here, and Wotan is little more than her vassal. He might have ignored that fact so far, but now there is no denying. The realization depresses him.

Wotan's Confession
(SCENE TWO)

Brünnhilde finds Big Daddy in a funk. The normally macho god is staring into space, gloomy and sad. That last fight with Fricka seems to have left him battered. He laments that he has been caught in his own trap. He, top dog and top god, suddenly sees that he is the least free of them all; a pitiable state!

Brünnhilde is shocked, for she has never seen him this depressed. But this was only the tip of the iceberg, for now he starts crying and lamenting in earnest: He is so, so sad, and the gods are in danger … The Valkyrie begs him to put his trust in her, to confide in her, for she will always be faithful.

Wotan looks at her, caresses her hair. Brünnhilde is his favorite daughter, the mistress of the banquet hall, the only one who is allowed to serve him food and drink. She embodies his true will, and thus he can tell her things that he would not tell anyone else. When he speaks to her, he actually speaks to himself; a soliloquy to reveal the truth: *What I tell no one verbally, remains unspoken for ever: I only talk to myself when I talk to you.*

If he told her his worries now however, wouldn't he contradict his own will? His daughter presses him to tell her whatever ails him. She confirms that, yes, she is his personified will. So finally the father of the gods confesses to her in a whisper: When he was young and obsessed with power, he entered into some agreements that harbored mischief. At the height of his power, he demanded love, even though he was never faithful. And then Alberich, the Nibelung, cursed love and won the Rhinegold and its attendant power. He, Wotan, tricked Alberich and stole the ring he had forged. He was forced to give that ring to Fasolt and Fafner in payment for the erection of the castle Walhall. Erda, wisest of the wise, warned him of the ring's dark power, but wouldn't explain further.

That had made him angry, and he descended into Erda's realm below the surface, using "*the magic of love*" to get her to tell him more. That seemed to work well enough, but he didn't like what she had to tell him: The gods would go down in ignominy. Incidentally, she also got pregnant from all this "magic of love," and bore Brünnhilde. Wotan then raised his daughter with eight of her sisters to be Valkyries—women he intended to help him change the course of history. He wanted to be prepared for when the enemy came, and therefore he sent them out to pick the best warriors from the battlefields, turning them into obedient soldiers for his defending army.

Brünnhilde interrupts him by stating that she has already collected a fair number of valiant fighters in Walhall. She thinks that he has nothing to worry about.

But Wotan's confession isn't over yet. In dramatic *sprechgesang*, he drones on: Erda warned him of Alberich's army, because the Nibelung wants revenge. Wotan would not be afraid of his hordes, unless the lord of darkness won back the ring he had forged. If Alberich ever got that ring back into his possession, Walhall would be doomed. Due to his curse, Alberich could use the magic of the ring to turn Wotan's warriors against their leader. The god would be defeated by his own soldiers.

This explains Wotan's desire to get his own hands on the ring again. Fafner, one of the two giants he paid with the cursed gold, is currently in possession of the hoard. He even killed his own brother to be the sole owner of the entire treasure. Wotan needs to take the ring from Fafner. The only problem is that that would violate the contract he made with the builders. Wotan's position as top god came into being through contracts; and thus he is a powerless slave to the contracts he made.

He goes on to explain that there is only one person who could do what he himself is not allowed to do: a free hero, not bound by any god's decrees or contracts, might accomplish what the god could not. His conundrum in this scheme however, is that he doesn't know how to *create* a being that then proceeds to do what Wotan wants, *but of his own account*. And thus, he concludes, it was all for naught: *For the Free man has to create himself; I can only create subjects to myself.* He is disgusted with this realization: "*What a predicament for a god!*"

Brünnhilde asks whether the Volsung Siegmund doesn't act of his own account, but Wotan shakes his head. The man is only protected by the sword, "*which a god's favor bestowed on him.*" He had lied to himself, thinking that this was the free hero he had been looking for. And now Fricka had seen through his self-deception, and had called his bluff. He must bend to her will.

He is convinced that, when he held Alberich's ring in his hands, its curse infected him: Now he is forced to leave what he loved, to kill whom he cherishes, and to betray those who trust him. The divine splendor that is Walhall is doomed to fall, and he is ready to give up his striving. He only wants one thing to happen: The end!

Alberich is going to take care of that, and he, Wotan, understands the meaning of Erda's prediction, now that it is too late: *"When Love's dark enemy begets a son in anger, the end of the Blessed ones will not be long delayed."* He heard that the Nibelung bought himself a wife and sired a son, the fruit of his hatred. How come the loveless elf could do this, while Wotan was unable to create a free man, even with all the love he put into this labor?

The god feels nothing but hatred for Alberich's offspring. He curses the dark elf's son, thus evoking the end of the gods: *What deeply revolts me I bequeath to you, the empty glory of divinity: greedily feed your hate on it!*

*

It is worth spending a few more moments on Erda's prophecy, because what is said here as an ominous announcement of the further course of the story is significant. Alberich gave a woman a lot of gold jewelry, and then proceeded to sire a son. The boy's name is Hagen, and he will play a sinister, decisive role in the third part of the *Ring*. Both the father of the gods and the elf beget sons who are meant to continue and fulfill their legacy. Alberich wants to retrieve the ring of power he forged from the Rhinegold. Wotan wants the ring so it doesn't fall into the elf's hands, sealing the fate of the godly tribe. Neither of them can achieve their goal themselves; they both need what the law today calls *vicarious agents*.

While Wotan used some nondescript woman from the woods to produce what Fricka calls *"your adultery's dissolute fruit,"* Alberich bought himself no less than a queen. She was the queen of the Gibichung, about whom we learn very little in the parts to come. We can only surmise what she was like by looking at what we learn about her other children: There is, for one, her son King Gunther, a real wuss, who needs the wiles and strength of his half brother Hagen in order to shine. In part four of the tetralogy, he voices his appreciation for said half brother by praising his mother's adulterous escapade that begot him. Then there is his moronic sister Gutrune, who seems to be grossly stupid and ugly, because they cannot find a suitable husband for her, and instead cover her in gold and frippery.

What's also interesting is that Fricka, in her function as goddess of matrimony, applies double standards: She hounds her own husband Wotan mercilessly because of his adultery, while turning a blind eye on the queen's tryst with Alberich. No call for consequences in their case. Thus the guardian of marriage is on her feet only when her own position of power is at stake.

*

Well, Wotan has already given up. He is denied what Fricka allows Alberich. His son is bound to die, while the elf's son may take his intended place in the story. In the face of this imbalance, Wotan sees his house of cards collapse. He anticipates the twilight of the gods. Brünnhilde is duly shocked by her father's confession. What is she supposed to do now? How can she assist Wotan? What does he want her to do?

Wotan sees no way out. He is caught between wishing and wanting, between marital frustration and reason of state. In the end, he takes back his original order and appoints Brünnhilde to be the fighter for Fricka's honor. He has taken that oath before his wife, and in the face of that, his own will becomes meaningless. Thus the Valkyrie is to fight on the side of Fricka's serf, Hunding.

Brünnhilde is stunned. She asks him to take back this last order. She knows how much the father loves this son, how much hope he had pinned on him. She wants to protect Siegmund, so Wotan's plans can still come to fruition. But the god cannot take it back; he orders her to fight on Hunding's side. He even warns her that it will not be an easy fight, because Siegmund is carrying a victorious blade, so she will have to bring all her cunning into this battle.

Brünnhilde rebels, for she was taught to love those that are dear to her father's heart as well. Thus she cannot and will not accept such an ambivalent order. What's more, she doesn't want to be Fricka's executor, for she embodies solely the true will of her father.

Wotan reacts like a cornered beast, snapping and biting. His blind rage is directed at Brünnhilde. He yells at her, insults her by saying that she, too, is nothing more than a creature of his will. He rants that he is so angry with the world he once loved, he can only warn anyone not to incite his wrath by opposing him now. No more backtalk! She is to execute what he charges her with: *Siegmund shall die. This is the Valkyrie's task.*

The music surges wildly, ebbing slowly until a gentle sadness remains. Brünnhilde stands numbly, trying to process what is going on. She has never seen her father like this. And now she is supposed to *"creep into this evil fight,"* support Hunding and send the Volsung to his doom? Even though it pains her greatly, is she really supposed to become disloyal and give up her former ward, whom Wotan saved by sending him to Hunding's cabin and showing him the magic sword in the first place? Brünnhilde is utterly baffled. What has her world come to?

On the Run
(SCENE THREE)

While Wotan confesses to his favorite daughter, and orders her to follow Fricka's wishes, helping Hunding to defeat his enemy, Siegmund and Sieglinde are on the run. Sieglinde feels shame for her incestuous fling with her own brother, while Siegmund ... well, he is a man. He sees only the desirable woman in his sister, and he feels all warm and tingly inside when he huffs and puffs about *"righteous anger"* and a sense of honor.

But now Siegmund wants to rest, whereas Sieglinde wants to march on. He takes her in his arms to soothe her fears. No more running he says, willing to face Hunding in a fight.

Sieglinde first hugs him tightly, but then a new train of thought leads her to ask her lover to leave her: She says she is dishonored and as good as dead. Hunding defiled her, and she obeyed him as her master, but never loved him. She sees herself as abject and undignified. All she has to offer is disgrace for her brother and ignominy for the suitor who awakened her love.

Siegmund tries to placate her. He intends to wash away her disgrace with Hunding's blood, avenging her honor with his

Nothung sword—literally, though that may have sounded like innuendo.

In the background, the horns of their pursuers are sounded. Hunding has woken from his deep sleep and immediately realized what was going on. He called his clan together, and now they are hunting the adulterers with bloodhounds. The wild barks and yelps echoes up to the heavens, where goddess Fricka as guardian of matrimony sits in her throne and watches Hunding's hunting party rush through the forest. Panicking, Sieglinde throws herself against Siegmund's manly chest, suddenly sobbing and feverish. In a vision she sees the hounds descending on her lover, bringing him down, while the sword breaks to pieces and the mighty ash tree falls.

That vista is too much for the poor woman. With a cry she sinks to the ground, unconscious. Siegmund is alarmed, gently takes her in his arms and kisses her forehead.

Brünnhilde Defies her Orders
(SCENE FOUR)

While Siegmund is still taking care of the unconscious Sieglinde, Brünnhilde approaches on her horse and accosts him: *Siegmund, look at me. I am she whom you will follow soon.* The Volsung doesn't know the armored warrior woman, so he asks who she is. The Valkyrie explains that those who see her are doomed to die. On the battlefield she only shows herself to those who will be taken to Walhall, where he will soon meet the *"Lord of battles"* and a host of other fallen heroes.

Siegmund wants to know if he will also meet his father Volsa in Walhall, and she confirms that he will find his father there. Next he asks if he will be greeted by a woman in Walhall. The harbinger of death wants to whet his appetite, even offering her own services: *Desirable maidens abound there in splendor. Wotan's daughter will gladly give you your drink.*

Several religions promise their faithful some sort of paradise in the hereafter. For the devout Muslim, the Quran advertises doe-eyed, large-breasted *houris* that wait for them to be taken as virginal brides. In Germanic mythology, "*desirable maidens*" also await the brave, in this case the nine Valkyries Wotan sired. They offer drinking horns to the fallen heroes. Siegmund remains unconvinced, despite the waiting maidens. Will "*his sister and bride*" accompany him to Walhall? Brünnhilde shakes her head. No, Sieglinde will have to "*breathe the air of earth*" for a while longer.

Siegmund kisses the still-unconscious Sieglinde on the forehead again and tells the heavenly maiden to give his best regards to Wotan, Volsa, the dead heroes and the other maidens. He prefers to stay with Sieglinde and is not coming to the hero graveyard she pitched to him so nicely.

Brünnhilde becomes authoritative: She only showed herself to him because he will be going to Walhall soon, no way around that. While he is still alive, she can only invite him, not force him, but once he dies, he'll be on his way. She has come to tell him of his impending death, for Hunding is going to slaughter him in battle.

Siegmund laughs at her. That Hunding? Not strong enough. He will be the one to slaughter the hunter, so she should be prepared to take that man instead of him. He draws his sword, showing it off: *Do you know this sword? He who made it for me promised me victory.* Brünnhilde is not impressed. She knows more than he does, and thus replies soberly: *He who made it for you has now decreed your death.*

Shaken, Siegmund cradles Sieglinde in his arms. She has come to him for protection, and now he cannot help her, now he should leave her alone here? Shame on the one who first forged the sword for him, and now takes the victory away. He does not want to go to Walhall. He'd rather go to hell, the realm of the goddess of death, Hella.

The normally badass Valkyrie is stunned by his behavior. "*Everlasting bliss*" means less to him than this frail woman in his arms? Her value system is shaken by that possibility. To add insult to injury, Siegmund tells her that while she may look young and beautiful, her heart must be icy cold. He thinks she is only there to scorn him and make fun of his pain, so he sends her away.

The mounted warrior woman sees the predicament he is in, and offers to take Sieglinde into her own care. Siegmund refuses, for he'd rather kill his woman than give her up to an uncertain fate: *I and no other shall touch her purity while she lives.* Brünnhilde plays her final card, revealing that Sieglinde is pregnant from Siegmund. The unborn child must be saved! But the Volsung is raving, beyond rational thought. He draws the magic sword and seems ready to stab his sleeping bride: *Two lives smile on you here: take them, Nothung, precious sword, take them with one blow.*

Brünnhilde is stumped. What now? She feels compassion for the maddened lover and the young mother-to-be, so she changes her tune, desperate to prevent the impending murder: Alright, Sieglinde and Siegmund are to live! The Valkyrie promises to tip the balance of the battle in his favor. In order to win, he only needs to trust his magical sword.

Much more optimistic than a minute earlier, Siegmund watches her horse trot away. He is ready for this battle. Hunding's pack is approaching.

Siegmund's Death
(SCENE FIVE)

The forest is boiling: Hunding and the rest of the pursuers are coming. Men are yelling, weapons are clanking, horns are calling. Siegmund kisses his beloved sister on the forehead one last time. He hopes that she will wake up from her faint only after the fight is over. Then he goes to face the enemy, his sword drawn and ready.

At the same time, Sieglinde is caught in an awful nightmare. She remembers that day in her childhood, when Hunding's clan attacked her home and burned it to the ground. She calls out to her father in her haunted sleep, but when the disaster happened, he was out hunting with her brother. She calls out to Siegmund, too.

But the only thing her brother can hear now is Hunding's taunt: He dares him to come out and surrender, so he won't have to send the dogs after him. He also says that he has Fricka on his side.

Siegmund taunts him right back: Hunding should fight, instead of hiding behind a woman! He holds up the magical sword that he pulled from the ash in Hunding's cabin. And then the two men start hacking at each other. This is clearly a life-or-death battle. In a flash of bright light, Brünnhilde suddenly appears to protect Siegmund with her shield. She eggs him on: *Strike him, Siegmund! Rely on your sword.*

But in that moment, Wotan enters the fray, too. To save Fricka's honor, he breaks from the clouds in a glowing red light. The father of the gods has to interfere here, because his favorite Valkyrie refuses to fulfill his orders, assisting Siegmund instead of Hunding. Brünnhilde did not see that coming. She draws back in fright. And while the tubas give everything, Wotan hurls his spear in Siegmund's direction. The sword clashes with the god's spear and breaks into a million pieces. The wonderful, magical sword is no match for its creator's weapon of choice. Siegmund the demigod, son of the chief god, has just been sentenced and disarmed by his own father. Now all Hunding has to do is thrust his own spear into the chest of the unarmed opponent. Siegmund falls.

The first offspring of the hero race sired by Wotan dies by the intervention of his own father. The winner of this battle is a man entrenched behind Fricka's back. The better man was slaughtered, and the one who had the law on his side survives. Then darkness descends on the battlefield, as if the deed needed to be veiled. Under cover of the blackness, the Valkyrie collects the bits and pieces of the magical sword. Then she pulls Sieglinde up onto her horse and rushes off into the night with her.

The victorious fighter pulls the spear from the chest of the fallen enemy. It pains Wotan to see the corpse of his son, and to accept that he doomed him to die this way. He feels only disdain for Hunding: *Be off, slave. Kneel before Fricka; tell her that Wotan's spear avenged what caused her shame.* When he dismisses him with a contemptuous wave of his divine hand, Hunding falls dead to the ground. Maybe he was cursed with a weak heart.

Wotan is angry with himself for being forced to interfere in this battle. Whatever he starts, it seems to turn against him. Nothing goes as he planned it: Now the great sword, which he planted so providently in the ash tree in Hunding's cabin, is destroyed. His son Siegmund, whom he sired to win back the ring of power, lies dead on the ground. And to top it all off, his daughter Brünnhilde has rebelled against his orders. She should have done the dirty job in his stead, the job Fricka had saddled him with.

How much is left of his status, his authority as chief of chiefs? He quickly mounts his divine steed and follows the Valkyrie, bent on punishing her for her disobedience and the frustration she caused him. It's time for the second break in this production. Time to ponder the unusual psychological constellation Wagner has set up for his heroes.

ACT THREE

The Ride of the Valkyries
(PRELUDE AND SCENE ONE)

Where might those warlike amazons live, those women whose job it is to pick up fallen warriors and drag them to Walhall? Why, of course their home is an aerie on the highest peak of a forbidding mountain range, a place that can only be reached by flight, and is unattainable to the wanderer below. From that windy mountaintop, the Valkyries enjoy the wide view over the landscape below, a quality they need for the fulfillment of their job. As soon as some kind of strife starts up somewhere, they stand ready to pick out the strongest lads from the heap of corpses, and spirit them away to Walhall.

There the Valkyries transform themselves into ladies of easy virtue, who anticipate the chosen warriors' each and every wish. In this way they ensure that Wotan possesses an ever-growing army of revenants ready to defend the stronghold of the gods against the dark hordes of the Nibelung in the impending final battle.

Brünnhilde's sisters even have their own signature tune, a piece of rising and falling music, ruled by rushing strings and resounding winds. This is the *"Ride of the Valkyries"*, one of the more rousing pieces of Wagner's *Ring*. The tempestuous music makes it easy to envision the wild women roaring merrily through the air, looking for places where people clout each other, and where the blood flows like red rivers. All the musicians pitch in for this roaring song; even the often chronically underemployed percussionists bang their cymbals together like there's no tomorrow.

Gerhilde, Ortlinde, Waltraute and Schwertleite are alreday at home, welcoming the return of their sister Helmwige with their merry calls of "*Hoyotoho! Hoyotoho! Heiaha! Heiaha!*" Helmwige carries a slaughtered man at her saddle. She tells the others in her cheerful soprano that the dead guy is Sintolt from the clan of the Hegeling. She wants to park her mare next to Ortlinde's stallion, but the horse kicks at her, because across its back, it still carries the corpse of the Irming Wittig, who had been Sintolt's enemy in life. Gerhilde laughs at the animals' antics: *The warrior's quarrel even antagonizes the horses.*

Mezzo-soprano Waltraute, still on the lookout, announces the arrival of Siegrune, and further behind, Grimgerde and Rossweisse are galloping through the air with their own glorious prey, and their own yells of "*Hoyotoho!*" and "*Heiaha!*" They are greeted by their still-cheering sisters. Ortlinde recommends that they keep all the horses separate, "*until our heroes' hatred has calmed.*"

The eight sisters are still waiting for Brünnhilde, who is supposed to bring in the Volsung Siegmund. Then they intend to ride into Walhall together, to present the freshly plucked reinforcement for his troops. And here she comes; Siegrune has spied her on the horizon. But the women sense that something is not as it should be. Even from far away, Brünnhilde looks hounded, and her horse Grane is snorting with exertion. This is not the usual gallop of a Valkyrie; it is the ride of someone who is fleeing from a pursuer. And it is not a hero she carries across her saddle, it is a woman! The others start to get restless.

Brünnhilde rushes towards her sisters, pleading: *Give me protection and help in my great distress.* The eight girls react with panic. Who is their sister fleeing from? The Valkyrie admits:

"The father of battles is pursuing me!" She is talking of Wotan, whose favorite daughter she was only yesterday. Why would he hound her now? What did she do? Shocked, Ortlinde sees a thunderstorm drawing near from the north. It's the father of the gods, wrapped up in a thundercloud, rushing towards their aerie on his sacred steed. The sisters believe that Brünnhilde must be out of her mind.

But their fugitive sister hastens to explain her predicament: She had been told to take the victory away from Siegmund, her own (half) brother, but she disobeyed this divine order and protected him with her shield. So her father had to join the fray himself, and fell his son with his powerful spear. She then took Sieglinde and escaped with her. Now she hopes that her sisters will hide her from the angry god.

Well, the sisters are not inclined to do so, for they don't understand what got into her: What did the unfortunate sister do? Woe betide her, or whatever a choir of upset Valkyries will say. *Have you disobeyed Warfather's solemn orders, Brünnhilde?* They shake their heads in disbelief, while singing at the top of their register. Meanwhile a thundering Wotan is coming closer. Brünnhilde is desperate, asking one after the other of her sisters to borrow their horses, because Grane is too exhausted to go on. But all she gets in return is cold refusal. Her cowardly sisters don't want to rebel against their father, they want to obey him—it's what they know, what they were taught to do.

This is when Sieglinde finally awakens from her trance. She doesn't understand why she wasn't allowed to die together with her Siegmund, so they could be united in the end. She wants to perish, and asks Brünnhilde to thrust her sword into her heart, but the Valkyrie refuses, telling Sieglinde that she must live for love. Why? Because she is expecting a child by her lover, which must be saved: *"A Volsung is growing in your womb."*

At first, Sieglinde is frightened, more so because in the background, Wotan rumbles and roars with his approaching thunderstorm. But then she processes the happy news and changes her tune: She now asks the Valkyries to save her child and shield her from harm. Again, the warrior women refuse. Only Brünnhilde is gripped by sympathy for her plight, and advises her to flee towards the east, into the vast forest that Wotan fears. That forest is the current home to the giant Fafner, who has transformed himself into a dragon and now guards the hoard of the Nibelung in that shape, to defend Alberich's ring. The Valkyrie gives her a piece of the broken magical sword, and tells her: *The noblest hero in the world, woman, you are carrying in the shelter of your womb.* One day, she adds, this hero will carry the re-assembled magical sword. And lastly, she provides the unborn hero with a name: He shall be called Siegfried.

Touched, Sieglinde finds the time to sing an aria that is a hymn of gratefulness to Brünnhilde: *Oh, mightiest of miracles, most glorious of women.* Then she rushes off on foot in the general direction of the creepy forest. Not a moment later, Wotan can be heard yelling for Brünnhilde to come out. Her sisters form a protective circle around her, lest their fuming father spies her right away, and tears her to pieces in his unholy wrath.

Wotan Casts out Brünnhilde
(SCENE TWO)

Wotan wants to make an example of his disobedient daughter. He rants at his Valkyries in his bass-baritone: *"Where is Brünnhilde, where is the lawbreaker?"* The eight sisters try to placate their father, but he scorns them as a *"soft-hearted gaggle of females."* After all, he raised his daughters to be brave and wild beings with hard hearts, and now they dare whimper when he wants to punish disloyalty?

The father of the gods is not just angry; he is also disappointed in his favorite daughter. Like nobody else, Brünnhilde knew his innermost thoughts. His wanted child broke that bond, and scorned his commandment publicly by directing the weapon he had created against him. He is the one who gave Brünnhilde her life, her name, her shield and armor, but now she is cowardly hiding from her prosecutor to evade her punishment.

Nope, the accused will not be called a coward. She steps forward from the protective circle her sisters have formed: *Here I am, father: pronounce your punishment.* He replies in a thunderous voice that her actions have already determined her punishment. She used to be the *"agent of his wishes,"* but turned her wishes against him. As *"bearer of his shield"* she raised her shield against him. She was *"disposer of fates,"* but wanted to change the outcome of the battle against his orders. Lastly, she used to be the *"inspiration of heroes,"* but goaded the heroes on to turn against Wotan. From now on, she shall no longer be his agent or his Valkyrie. She is on her own.

Brünnhilde has not anticipated this verdict: Does Wotan intend to cast her out?

He clarifies: He no longer wants to see her in Walhall; she is fired from her job of bringing in fallen heroes. No more presiding over his banquet hall, no more handing him his drinking horn as his personal cupbearer. Yes, she shall be cast out from the eternal clan of the gods. In short: he never wants to lay eyes on her again!

The remaining eight Valkyries break into their melodic lamentation, bewailing the fate of their sister. Wotan cannot be swayed however, and he bans Brünnhilde from the Valkyrie rock. She shall fall into a magical sleep and belong to the first man who finds her in this state.

The other Valkyries wail even louder than before: Shall Brünnhilde really become mortal, a woman whose youth will fade and who will wither and die in the arms of a mere man? That would be a crying shame, and a blight on the entire race of the Valkyries.

Wotan stands firm and proclaims Brünnhilde's expulsion from the community of her sisters. No more riding through the air on her horse either. All her divine privilege will be taken from her, and from now on, she will have to obey a different master: a human man, who will make her a housewife. Brünnhilde is doomed, and her sisters shall stay away from her. If any of them stands with her against his explicit will, acting as foolishly and spitefully as she did, they will meet the same fate.

The normally brave Valkyries don't need to be told twice. They scream and hastily mount their horses, rushing off in headless flight. Brünnhilde breaks down. The thunderstorm subsides, and the woodwinds prelude the farewell of the two divine beings. The wistful strings join them in their plangent announcement of nightfall.

The Ordeal
(SCENE THREE)

Wotan and Brünnhilde are alone. The father has lost some of his power and standing. His wife has shown him the boundaries of his divine might, and shown herself to be the true mistress on the throne of the gods. Siegmund, the son he sired to recapture the ring of power, has fallen victim to Fricka's anger. The magical sword Nothung, which he forged and then thrust into the trunk of the world ash tree, is nothing more than a puzzle of steel. His favorite daughter Brünnhilde has defied him and become a rebel. The entire estate of the gods is out of joint after all of this. None of his maneuvers, tricks and lies has yielded the intended result. If Wotan wants to save face—and thus his position—he needs to keep up appearances and overthrow the insurrection: Brünnhilde must be punished for her disobedience, even if it breaks her father's heart.

To make matters worse, his daughter starts a discussion on the question of guilt and responsibility: She says that she fulfilled the order he gave her as Lord of Walhall, assisting Siegmund in the battle. Wotan disagrees, for he revoked his original order and gave her a new one. But Brünnhilde insists: *When Fricka made your own intentions foreign to you, when you took her point of view, you were your own enemy.* From her point of view, Wotan gave her the second order only to placate his wife Fricka. She does not believe that he truly seconds the goddess' decision.

At the same time, Brünnhilde knows how dearly Wotan loved his son. She knows his dilemma and feels his pain. Thus as his alter ego, she shielded the young hero. She had Wotan's back, seeing what he didn't want to see. She also felt Siegmund's emotions, and experienced firsthand what he meant when he felt "*unbounded love's terrible sorrow.*" This consonance caused her cold heart to awaken to love; she understood the Volsung and decided that he must win instead of die. Thus she defied her father's commandment.

Wotan knows that the Valkyrie did what his heart would have wanted to do. He tries to justify his actions, claiming that necessity forced him to alter his decision. He throws in reason of state, the fragile peace among the divine family, "*when desperate necessity had roused my anger.*" And then he accuses Brünnhilde of surrendering to "*heavenly emotion,*" and thus renouncing him. Therefore he will have to shun her in the future.

Brünnhilde made her decision based on a gut reaction. She loved the one her father had loved. If Wotan chooses to banish her now, he will split his self in the process. So be it, but she requests that he does not humiliate her further, for that would debase him in turn: If she must belong to some imperious man as part of her punishment, at least that man should be worthy. One might wonder whether she already envisions the offspring of Siegmund and Sieglinde as her suitor, especially given that the chords of the Volsung motif can be heard at this point. Brünnhilde pleads: *Let my sleep be protected by terrors that scare, so that only a fearless unrestrained hero may one day find me here on the rock.*

Wotan wants to be done with this awkward situation, so he grants her this wish. He sings a song of farewell, and promises—accompanied by the ardent, roaring orchestra—that "*a bridal fire shall burn for you,*" which will deter all cowardly suitors. *For only one shall win the bride, one freer than I, the God!* He summons Loge, who happens to be the god of fire, and this wily assistant surrounds the rock (on which the Valkyrie falls into a deep sleep) with an insurmountable ring of fire. Wotan gives his favorite daughter one last look, seals off the rock and chants his incantation: *Whosoever fears the tip of my spear shall never pass through the fire!*

The Valkyrie's fate is sealed. Cast out from the realm of the gods, banned from Walhall, expulsed from her own father, she must lie like Sleeping Beauty until some bold warrior kisses her awake. But who could that be? What man is free and strong enough to laugh in the face of the tip of Wotan's spear, and to blaze a trail through the ring of fire?

"*Siegfried*," the next part of *The Ring of the Nibelung*, will tell us more about this exceptional hero. Brünnhilde is in for a long, long wait, dreaming of her savior. Because as we know, Siegfried is currently growing from Siegmund's seed in Sieglinde's womb. It will be at least twenty years before the boy is ready to save ladies from fiery circles. Thankfully the audience can fast forward, and learn the further course of the story after an extended pause, in the third part.

SIEGFRIED

Second day of the scenic festival *The Ring of the Nibelung*

First performance:
Bayreuth, Festspielhaus
August 16, 1876

Characters in "Siegfried"

Siegfried, a foundling raised in a forest blacksmith shop by the dwarf Mime, rebels against his foster father.

Mime, deceitful blacksmith dwarf, covets the ring of power.

The Wanderer, earthly persona of the restless and maybe moribund chief of the gods, Wotan, who is determined to stay on top of things.

Alberich, former leader of the black elves from the subterranean kingdom of Nibelheim, lies in wait in front of Fafner's lair, hoping for an opportunity to seize the ring he once forged.

Fafner, last Lord of the Giants (nope, not the New York ones. Real giants), guards the magic ring in the shape of an almost invincible dragon, into which he transformed himself with the help of a magic helmet-cloak-thingie.

Erda, primeval world mother, asked by Wotan what fate has in store for him and the rest of the gods, persuaded to have casual sex with Wotan, which resulted in their daughter Brünnhilde.

Brünnhilde, Wotan's daughter and formerly his favorite Valkyrie, but because of her disobedience banned to the top of a rock that is surrounded by a ring of fire.

Waldvogel, little birdie whose song Siegfried learns to understand after he imbibed dragon's blood.

ACT ONE

The Smithy in the Forest
(PRELUDE)

The orchestra commences with more than five minutes worth of a muffled mumbling and grumbling, slowly swelling, nebulous, restrained. Winds and strings put the listeners in the mood by coaxing the deepest possible notes from their instruments. They reiterate the sinister and ghastly backstory of the *Ring of the Nibelung*.

A bassy B flat minor describes the subterranean kingdom where Alberich rules the elven tribe. Here in Nibelheim the dwarf lord hoarded the stolen gold he robbed from the Rhine daughters. Here, too, the despot coerced his brother into forging the magical ring of power, as well as the magic helmet that allows its bearer to transform into anything he wants.

We hear the rhythmic hammering of the goldsmith. We feel with Mime, as he felt the whip his brother was swinging across his back, as he was longing for a chance to escape. Well, his chance would come, for Alberich fell into the hands of robbers, too—he was outwitted by Wotan and his minion Loge! They seized and bound him, and took the entire hoard from him, to use it to pay off the giants Fasolt and Fafner for their services as builders of the Walhall stronghold.

Under cover of the ensuing ruckus, Mime fled Alberich's kingdom. Drawn by the lure of the golden ring, he moved his smithy deep into an enchanted forest. This choice of location was in no way random, for in this forest, the giant-turned-dragon Fafner guards both ring and stolen gold, and the greedy gnome Mime wants to have and enjoy both to himself. Bass and contrabass tuba describe this terrible place.

The Foster Son of the Dwarf
(SCENE ONE)

As the curtain rises, Mime is busy in his workshop. The fire in the forge is blazing, the chimney is smoking, the bellows are hissing. In a mad frenzy, the dwarf is beating down on a glowing piece of iron, swearing loudly in a litany of grievances: The best weapon he ever made was snapped in half by the "contemptuous boy," as if it was a mere toy sword. This rouses our curiosity. Who is this boy Mime complains about? A boy whose childish strength only one piece of steel could withstand: the magical sword Nothung? Despite his great skill, Mime finds himself unable to put the pieces of that legendary sword back together.

Too bad, because it is the only weapon that might kill Fafner, who dwells in *Neidhöhle* (literally: cave of envy) in the shape of a "*fearsome dragon*" and guards the treasure of the Nibelung. As usual, Mime appears desperate. He feels the same coercion he endured under his brother Alberich, only this time it is a mere teenager who demands that he forge a suitable weapon for the all-too-strong young upstart. In time with the music, the dwarf hammers away angrily at the metal.

And here comes the "boy" in question: Siegfried, son of the twins Siegmund and Sieglinde, has grown up to be a hooligan of a guy, developing an immense physical strength in this remote, stark place. He lives according to his own set of rules, free from duties and demands. Right now, he is dragging a captured bear on a leash onto the stage.

Mime is frightened by the animal and hides behind his forge. What does the uncouth lad want with the wild beast anyway? Siegfried laughs at him: He brought the shaggy animal along to put more pressure behind his request for a sword; he has been waiting far too long for his weapon. Mime hastens to show him his newest piece, still glowing from the forge. The young Hercules releases the captured animal with a pat on its back, and Mime reappears from his hiding place, lamenting again: He does like bear meat alright, but the living, breathing beast gives him the creeps.

The young man is greatly amused by the old coward, and tells him that he was roaming the woods in search of a better companion than him. When he blew his horn, the bear answered his call with a growl of his own. So he bound and brought him here in order to add authority to his demand for a decent weapon.

Reluctantly the blacksmith hands him the blade he had been working on. He is very proud of his latest work, but the youngster scorns his efforts: *"Do you call this puny pin sword?"* He bangs the staff against the anvil, where is breaks into pieces in a shower of sparks. He calls the dwarf a *"base bungler,"* who keeps raving about giants, battles and heroic deeds, but cannot even forge a sharp enough toothpick. Siegfried is ready to finish his foster father: It would be best to split his skull right now, so this sad spectacle would come to an end.

Mime just keeps on whining and wailing: The boy is always roughhousing, and he is ungrateful, keeps forgetting the good that was done to him. Why can't he obey the one who has been taking care of him, old Mime? The gnome brings in a roast on a spit, together with a mug of sauce. Maybe the young man is hungry? But the presumptuous young hoodlum raises a fuss and throws the grub at Mime's head: *"Meat I've roasted for myself: swallow your swill alone!"*

The old gnome ups the ante. He lists all the things he has done for the ingrate: raised him from an infant's age; fed, clothed, housed the "*little mite*" and kept him warm. He has been doing all the housework, while the "*hasty boy*" spends his days roaming the forest. He has been the boy's teacher, providing him with knowledge and sharpening his wits. What does he get in return for all his efforts? Ridicule, scorn, and—yes—hatred!

Siegfried looks at him thoughtfully. He will admit that he learned a lot from Mime, but the one thing he never learned was to love Mime. Quite the contrary: When his foster father brings in food and drink, all he feels is repulsion. When he prepares Siegfried's bed, sleep is elusive. And when he tries to teach him how to be witty, he prefers to remain deaf and dumb. He even feels the urge to grab him by the back of his neck and twist it! Any animal in the forest means more to him than the goblin before him; he cannot understand why he keeps returning to the nasty dwarf anyway.

Uh-oh, the young boy is trying to figure out who he really is. The elf tries to suck up to him: *My child, that teaches you to know how dear I am to your heart.* He entreats the teenager to rein in his wild nature, and learn to love him: *What the bird is to the fledgling when it feeds it in the nest before the fledgling can fly: such to you, my lad, is sage, attentive Mime - such he must be!*

Siegfried laughs off the argument. Does Mime want to take him for a fool? In spring, he often observed those twittering birdies: Male and female ones, cavorting, building some sort of nest or shelter, sitting there brooding until their young started to test their little wings. Even wolves and wild foxes he has seen appear in pairs. The male brought food to the nest where the female was feeding the cubs. So the logical question is: Where is Mime's *"loving wife, that I may call her mother?"*

The dwarf dismisses the question and calls Siegfried a fool. Is he a bird or a fox? Duh! But the boy repeats his sermon of all the things he did for him, asking: *"Did you really make me without a mother?"*

The grumpy old gnome is running out of arguments in this discussion of the birds and the bees. He demands that the boy simply accepts that he has been both father and mother to him. Period. Of course Siegfried doesn't buy it. He has seen his mirror image in a brook, and couldn't find any likeness to Mime: *As like as a toad and a glittering fish; but a fish never had a toad for a father!* And with this thought comes the realization: Now he knows why he keeps coming back! He wants to know from his foster father who his real parents are. Mime tries to placate, to evade, but to no avail: Siegfried takes him into a headlock and threatens to beat the truth out of him.

The gnome whelps and begs for his life. To the sounds of the Volsung motif he admits that he is neither father nor relative to the boy, yet Siegfried still owes everything he is and knows to him, Mime. Once upon a time the dwarf found a whimpering woman in the woods. He brought the pregnant lady to his cave and helped her give birth to an infant she called Siegfried (and here a horn sounds the corresponding remembrance motif), which she then left in his care. Before she closed her eyes forever, she told him whence she got the name: The Valkyrie Brünnhilde told her the name, after she had saved her from the deadly battle between Hunding and Siegmund.

Mime is afraid that Siegfried will beat him up, so he falls back into his litany of good deeds, but the boy is impatient and wants to know the whole truth. He interrupts the squawking gnome and demands to know the name of his mother. Mime professes to have forgotten what it was, and Siegfried is ready to slap some sense into him. Alright, alright, so his mom was called—Sieglinde!

He won't tell him the name of his dad, though, saying that all he knows is that he fell on the battlefield. Then Mime tries to placate his foster son with his old lullaby, but the lad is suspicious of the lying old goblin. Does he have proof of his story?

The blacksmith ponders that question for a moment, before showing the boy some pieces of metal: *Your mother gave me this: for my pains, feeding and attention she left this as paltry payment. Look here, a shattered sword! She said your father carried it when he fell in his last fight.*

Siegfried is thrilled. The old man shall put these pieces back together, for they will form a strong sword; exactly the kind of weapon the boy has been looking for! He tells Mime to do it today, or else he will give him a beating. And then he plans to leave, walk out into the world, never to return. The dwarf is not his dad, so his hut is not his home. He will fly away, free as a bird, oh yes! Intoxicated by this prospect of freedom, Siegfried rushes off into the woods, singing. The orchestra accompanies him with a lively tune.

The gnome is stumped. What to do? He cannot put the pieces of the old sword together. The legendary blacksmith skills of the people from underground fail in the face of the unknown material. He sees his hopes dashed: He wanted to lure the boy to Fafner's lair, so the young Hercules could slaughter the dragon and bring him the golden ring. This is the prize he had hoped to gain from raising the kid as his own: Siegfried's strength was supposed to gain him the ring and the rest of the treasure, so he could become Lord and Master of the world. That would also have given him a chance to get back at his tyrannical brother.

The last twenty years have been spent preparing this plan, and now everything seems lost: *Niblung hatred, trouble and toil will not knit Nothung together for me, nor weld the sword into a whole!* Despondent, Mime stares at his anvil. He sees no way out of his dilemma, but just then, fate comes a-knocking in the guise of a wanderer …

A Life-or-Death Wager (Scene Two)

Mime is startled by a scary figure that steps out from the dark fir forest into the light of his one-man iron and steel business. He wears a long cloak in midnight blue and uses a spear for a walking staff. On his head sits a hat with a wide brim, but the wary dwarf notices that the old visitor is missing one eye.

Step by step, the stranger comes closer to the artisan, who wants to know just who comes looking for him in his remote corner of the woods. "*The world calls me Wanderer,*" the old one introduces himself in a deep bass. Well then, wander on and good riddance, the gnome thinks, for he already has enough on his mind, and is in no mood to play the gracious host: *I want to be alone and apart: I let loiterers go their way.*

But the unwelcome guest is not easily deterred. He lets his eyes roam the hut, steps over to the fire in the forge, and spies the pieces of the broken sword Nothung. In one glance, he understands the blacksmith's worries, as well as his inability to recreate the sword. He has come to make the best of the mess he created. Because the old wanderer is none other than Wotan himself, and he literally has an iron in this fire in the deep dark woods.

He whispers into the dwarf's ear: *Many imagined they were wise but knew not what they needed; I let them ask for guidance and gave my counsel as guerdon.* Mime thinks that something is definitely fishy about this guy, not the least because he uses such strange diction: "guerdon" is an archaic word for "reward." But the more pressing question is: What does the creepy stranger want? The dwarf doesn't suspect that he is face to face with the chief god, whom he met decades before in his former home Nibelheim, Neither does he know that his weird visitor is battling his frustration with marital quarrel and misguided politics by doing what his wife Fricka hates most: roaming the earth. Mime wouldn't care even if he knew all that; all he wants is to be rid of the guy.

He is inhospitable; he tells the wanderer that he knows enough and doesn't need additional "wisdom," but Wotan merely scoffs at him, pointing to the broken pieces of metal in the forge. Then he sits down and challenges Mime as if he were a quiz show host on cable TV: If the blacksmith really thinks he is that wise, the wanderer will wager his own head in a test of knowledge. If he fails to correctly and sensibly answer three random questions, Mime can have his head.

The dwarf senses that the only way to get rid of the annoying guest is to give him some really difficult riddles to solve. Alright, he is ready, grinning and rubbing his hands in expectation. First he wants to know what tribe calls the center of the earth its home—surely someone who has wandered far and wide must know this? The old man smirks and looks the miserable goblin up and down, before answering in his deep voice: Why, it's the Nibelung, and their subterranean kingdom is called Nibelheim. They are black elves, and Black Alberich is their former master. The potentate possessed a magical ring, with which he coerced his subjects to collect and hoard a mountain of shimmering treasure, planning to buy lordship over all the world, but then his empire broke apart.

Mime stares at the wanderer in surprise. How come this man knows so much about his tribe? Well, he simply needs to find a more difficult topic for his second question. Alright, if his guest knows everything about the world below the surface, what about those who live on the "*face of the earth*?" The dwarf chuckles to himself, because only few people know anything about this nearly extinct race.

The omniscient Wotan doesn't need to think twice: "*On the earth's face flourishes the race of giants,*" and their home is called Riesenheim. Its chieftains Fasolt and Fafner envied Alberich his great power, so they seized his treasure, including the magical ring. Then a quarrel sprung up between the brothers, resulting in Fafner killing Fasolt. The former has been guarding the gold in the guise of a dragon ever since.

The blacksmith is stunned by the intimate knowledge of things that very few beings know. His visitor is already waiting for the third question, pointing his staff in the direction of the hearth, where the pieces of the broken sword gleam in the fire. He expects the dwarf to ask who can recast this metal into a sword again, because that is the crucial gap in Mime's knowledge. It is also the sole reason why Wotan suggested this wager in the first place.

The god knows that only the Volsung Siegfried, Mime's foster son and his own grandson, is able to slaughter the dragon with the help of the sword Nothung. Siegfried's feat would also be Wotan's last chance of getting the powerful gold ring back into his possession, and thus prevent the looming twilight of the gods. He seems to take it for granted that his grandson would place the recaptured ring at his feet.

The dwarf blacksmith however is caught up in the web of his own thoughts, so he doesn't see the obvious. Instead of asking about the sword, he wants to know: If the Nibelung dwell below ground, and the giants above it, who is enthroned in the heavens?

The old man with the slouch hat rises to his full height, ramming his spear into the ground so hard that the entire hut starts shaking. He roars at the frightened black elf: *In the cloudy heights live the gods: Walhall is their dwelling. They are spirits of light, and Wotan, Lord of Light, rules over them.* The chief god made a weapon for himself from a branch of the World Ash Tree, emblem of his rule. Its shaft is carved with runes of sacred alliance and loyalty contracts. He who holds this spear holds the world together; Nibelung as well as giants must obey its bearer for all eternity. And with that, he sits down again and stares at the trembling gnome with his one eye.

Mime has had his chance. He asked his three questions, and they were all answered. Wotan shakes his head at the folly of his host: He should have asked something he really could use, but he doesn't even know what that is, even though his guest put his life at stake. Well, as tradition would have it, the dwarf's head is his if Mime cannot answer *his* three questions in return.

By now the slow little blacksmith has realized who entered his hut: *Wotan's eyes fell on me, peered into my cave: before him my mother-wit melts away.* He says he hopes that he is wise enough to quite literally keep his head. Out with the questions!

Wotan makes himself comfortable at the dwarf's table. His first question is about his own kin: *Which is the race that Wotan oppressed and yet whose life is dearest to him?* Mime hops up and down with glee, for he knows the answer to that one. The Volsung are the tribe which Wotan put into this world, which he loved dearly, yet treated them badly. Siegmund and Sieglinde, the twins, sprang from the divine bloodline. They begot the strongest Volsung offspring, Siegfried.

The wanderer is visibly impressed. What a clever guy Mime is! Then the answer to his second question shouldn't be a problem either: A wise Nibelung is said to be raising the boy, preparing him for killing Fafner and bringing home the ring. But what kind of sword does the boy need to slaughter the dragon Fafner?

Easy-peasy, the gnome thinks. He knows the answer: *Nothung*! The steel's name is Nothung! A long time ago, Wotan thrust it into the trunk of the ash tree, where it waited for the one man who could pull it out. The strongest heroes failed to do so, until Siegmund came and pulled it out. He used it to fight, but then it broke when it was hit by Wotan's spear. Ever since, a clever blacksmith has been keeping the pieces. And this blacksmith is also the only one who knows *that only with the Wotan sword will a brave but stupid boy, Siegfried, slay the dragon.*

The wanderer applauds. Irony rife in his voice, he proclaims Mime the cleverest of the clever. Hence the third question will be just as easy for him: *Tell me, wily weapon-smith: who will weld the sturdy splinters of the sword Nothung?*

The dwarf is startled. He tears at his hair, runs around in hectic circles. When he realizes that he cannot solve this riddle, he is suddenly very scared. He deemed himself the most skillful of all artisans, but here he is at the end of his wits. He cannot fix or forge the steel. He has already tried many times, but his tools failed him. Only a miracle can save him now!

The mysterious visitor stands and stares into the fire. Three times the goblin had the chance to find out what he really wants to know, and yet he couldn't think of a useful question. Instead he asked about faraway worlds. Mime senses that his guest knows the answer to the crucial question. He hits the panic button: He squandered his life in this wager. At least Wotan is going to give him the coveted answer: „*Only one who has never felt fear shall forge Nothung anew.*" Then the father of the gods shows his magnanimous side: He won't take the dwarf's head today. Instead he gives it to the one who has never felt fear. Of course he is thinking of fearless Siegfried.

The wanderer disappears into the woods without another word. Shaken to the core, Mime sinks to the ground. What now? He stares off into space and senses that his end is near. He is doomed!

The Magical Sword
(SCENE THREE)

Haunted by the dark prophecy of doom, the dwarf blacksmith sees specters all around him. A furious, passionate soundscape, like a musical painting, describes the state he is in. Lights flare, flicker, twinkle and shimmer around him. From the dark fir underbrush, we can hear growling, roaring and seething sounds. A terrible maw gapes, ready to devour Mime: Fafner the dragon wants to swallow him whole. Hounded by such visions, the gnome cowers in the corner of his hut like a picture of misery as Siegfried comes home.

He hears the boy call out for him: *Ho there! Mime, you coward! Where are you? Where are you hiding?* Trembling with fear, the dwarf asks whether his foster son has come alone. Siegfried laughs at him. Why is the master smith hiding behind his anvil? Is he sharpening the steel? Mime crawls out, bewildered, mumbling, deranged. The steel? How could he weld it together? The wanderer has told him that only the man who never knew fear can forge Nothung anew, but that is also the man who is going to kill him! In his frantic logic, that means that the rebellious teen that lives under his roof must learn what fear is, and quickly, otherwise Mime will be dead in a bit.

So the foster-father announces hesitantly that in the boy's absence, he learned what fear was, in order to pass this crucial bit of knowledge on to his son. The mightiest sword would be useless, Mime claims, if its bearer knows no fear. He says that he promised Siegfried's mother on her deathbed to send her offspring out into the world only after he has learned what the heebie-jeebies are. That was Sieglinde's last wish!

Siegfried rants at him that if fear is such an important skill, why hasn't he mastered it yet? The dwarf asks him in a whisper: Has he never felt a *"grim horror grip his limbs,"* when out and about in the dark forest? Has his heart never beaten in his throat at the sound of eerie noises in the night? Has he never trembled in the face of dancing will-o'-the-wisps? Has he never sensed an impending disaster in the black woods, sending a shiver down his spine?

The nature boy ponders these questions for a moment, but he cannot remember ever experiencing a feeling such as the ones Mime has just described. So far, he has roamed the woods without knowing fear. Trees, plants and animals have been his friends. But he will gladly learn the art of being afraid, if Master Mime, this miserable coward, can teach him.

Cunningly, the gnome tells him that at the eastern end of the forest, a dangerous dragon dwells close to the *Neidhöhle*, the cave of envy. This monster has already strangled and devoured many men, and its aspect alone is sufficient to teach anyone what fear is. Siegfried is excited; he wants to leave immediately to see for himself. The blacksmith must finally repair his sword, and quickly. Mime starts up his usual whining singsong, claiming that his strength is not sufficient to conquer the magic of the steel. Only the man who does not know fear might be able to do it.

When Wagner wrote this scene in the fall of 1856, he was living in a city apartment in Zurich, Switzerland. The composer suffered gravely from the street noise. In his autobiography *My Life* he wrote about the situation: *A tinker had established himself opposite our house, and stunned my ears all day long with his incessant hammering. In my disgust at never being able to find a detached house protected from every kind of noise, I was on the point of deciding to give up composing altogether until the time when this indispensable condition should be fulfilled. But it was precisely my rage over the tinker that, in a moment of agitation, gave me the theme for Siegfried's furious outburst against the bungling Mime. I played over the childishly quarrelsome Polter theme in G minor to my sister, furiously singing the words at the same time, which made us all laugh so much that I decided to make one more effort.* (Excerpt quoted from the English edition provided by Project Gutenberg: www.gutenberg.org)

Anyway, Siegfried pushes the dwarf aside and takes over the anvil. The blacksmith chides him, saying he has been a lazy apprentice, and doesn't know how to forge a good weapon. The boy tells the grouch to get lost, or else he might end up in the fire "by accident." He places the pieces in a vice and files them down, until he has a heap of shavings. Mime whines that this procedure will wear down his precious tools. He's never seen such dumb work. In the meantime, the fire in the forge is flaring up higher and higher. Siegfried works the bellows, making the charcoal glow. He belts out a wild song as he makes the sparks fly.

Mime watches his antics from a safe distance, and suddenly the scales fall from his eyes: Now he knows what the wanderer was talking about! None other than fearless Siegfried will forge the necessary sword and stab Fafner with it. Then he will seize the treasure of the Nibelung, and become the new Lord of the Ring. The dwarf's life would be forfeited. Panicking, he ponders how he can save himself, and get his hands on the magical ring at the same time. He will have to use cunning, of course: Mixing a sleeping potion to serve the conqueror of the worm after the battle seems like a good idea. Once the boy is asleep, he can kill him easily and grab the precious stuff. He could never win in an open fight, but poison, the weapon of cowards, could work to his advantage.

The youthful muscle man is oblivious to the dwarf's evil plans. While working at the crucible, he sings about the steps he is following. The glowing mass of molten shavings is poured into a staff-shaped cast, and then quenched with cold water. The resulting staff is thrust into the embers of the forge once again, making it sweat. He belts out his praise for the emergent sword: *"Nothung, Nothung, trusty sword!"*

In a letter, Wagner called his belting songs "very peculiar songs." These singing parts come close to what the opera world would call an aria, but the composer didn't think much of those. He intended to create his own kind of song. The word *heldentenor* (translated as heroic tenor, or better, as protagonist tenor) has come to signify a special type of tenor voice, more "heavy" and carrying than your usual lyrical tenor, but it also means quite squarely the kind of voice, song and attitude that Siegfried embodies here.

Meanwhile, the young Hercules is triumphantly belting out a hymn to his own creative power and joy. Mime seems delirious, screeching about some future Master of the Universe. From the corner of his eye, the youth watches the old man's antics, shaking his head at the dwarf's new tack: Mime has jumped up and is mixing a strange brew from a bunch of herbs. Oh, is the great artisan taking up cooking because he is fed up with hammering? He broke all of his worthless swords, and he doesn't even want to know what the crazy crone is brewing now, and he certainly doesn't want to try it.

The warrior-to-be bullies the red-hot steel, hitting hard to form and forge his weapon. Then he proceeds to fasten the blade to its hilt, testing Nothung by slicing the air. Then he sharpens the blade again. The dwarf's mood is getting better and better, for he can already see himself wear the ring of power on his finger. He jumps around with his freshly brewed bottle of sleeping potion, fantasizing about his bright future: He is going to subdue his brother Alberich, who once made him a slave. The disdained dwarf will become the revered new Lord of the Nibelung. He will be King, Leader of the Elves, Master of the Universe, all with capital letters! The world will bow to him, tremble before his wrath. Gods and heroes will clamor for trinkets from his hoard, and grovel at his feet, oh yes. The two songs, Siegfried's and Mime's, overlap and interfere with each other.

And now Siegfried has finished his job. He swings his sword, rejoicing: *Nothung, Nothung, trusty sword! Now you are fixed in the hilt. You were broken, but I made you whole; no stroke shall ever again shatter you.* He turns to the incapable blacksmith and shows him how well his steel works. With a single blow, he cuts the anvil in half. There is a mighty crash, and the orchestra riots. Mime faints with fright, dropping to the floor.

Confidently, the youthful fighter raises his sword high. As if he had cut the rope right through when he cut the anvil, the curtain rushes down, too. Fafner, the man in dragon form, is going to feel the heat …

ACT TWO

The Ring Wanders on
(PRELUDE)

There are various theories about the origin of dirty corners. One of the more well-known says that as soon as anything is thrown away into a corner, more garbage accrues automatically. The same mechanism may apply to bars, brothels and robbers' caves: They are as attractive to the respective milieu as light is to moths.

The *Neidhöhle*, or cave of envy, is located in the easternmost corner of the ancient forest, and it exudes a comparable magical pull: The dwarf blacksmith Mime transferred his one-man workshop into the forest. His foster son Siegfried grew up in these woods. Wotan, chief of the gods, roams the tangled wilderness in his flight from his wife Fricka and from his own plans gone awry, dressed up as an old wanderer. Even Alberich, who got the ball rolling with his theft of the Rhinegold, has been lying in wait next to the entrance of the cave for decades, waiting for his chance. What draws all these people to this forest, and this hole in the ground? Well, the cave is inhabited by Fafner, the last survivor of the race of giants.

Fafner guards the cursed Nibelung gold, which he received from Wotan for the building of Walhall, before he slaughtered his brother Fasolt out of enviousness. With the help of the magic helmet that Mime forged, the last lord of the race of giants took on the form of a bloodthirsty dragon. He kills anyone that dares pester him, and is said to be nearly invincible. Only a free hero that holds the magical sword Nothung could defeat him. And as it happens, such a man is currently trotting through the forest, in search for the dragon's lair, while the trombones blare on about the curse of the gold. Yes, Siegfried is on his way.

In front of the Cave of Envy
(SCENE ONE)

Alberich keeps watch in front of the cave, his eyes on the entrance. Suddenly a heavy wind springs up. Did he just see a bright horse rush through the forest? Is the dragonslayer finally coming? The light expires as quickly as it appeared.

The clouds disperse and the moon bathes the arrival in its wan light: It is Wotan, the wanderer. Alberich recognizes him from Nibelheim, when he and his pal Loge stole the treasure and the magic ring from him, in order to pay off the builders of Walhall. He hisses angrily at the god: *Be off, you shameless thief! Are you searching around for more mischief?*

The man with the slouch hat is amused: Is the black elf standing guard at Fafner's lair? As for himself, he merely came to look around; he is out hiking. Alberich doesn't buy it. He spits out a mirthless laugh and warns Wotan that he is no longer as dumb as when he let them take away his ring all those years ago. He knows quite well that Wotan paid the builders with his treasure, carving the runes of the contract into his staff. With a breach of that contract, the spear would break and become worthless. That is the reason why the god cannot simply go in and seize the gold from Fafner.

The wanderer takes a menacing step towards the dwarf. He reminds him that he did not make a contract with Alberich, but defeated him with his strength and cunning. And he says he keeps the spear for warfare, nothing else. The dwarf lord taunts him, for he knows that the keeper of the hoard is doomed, due to the curse he himself has put on the gold. Thus he thinks that Wotan is very much afraid of the power falling back into the hands of a Nibelung. Because as soon as the magic ring was in his, Alberich's, possession again, he would know how to make use of its power, contrary to the dumb giants. With the help of an army from hell, he would storm Walhall, break the reign of the gods, and enthrone himself as master.

The man in the moonlight smiles. He knows Alberich's malicious plans, but he isn't worried at all, because the ring will soon be held by the man who wins it in straightforward battle. Alberich had better be wary of his own brother, instead of focusing on Wotan. Because as they speak, Mime is leading the boy that is supposed to defeat Fafner towards the cave. That boy has no idea about either his divine ancestry or the ring, but Alberich's brother Mime knows exactly what he is doing.

The dwarf is skeptical. Wotan is not interested in seizing the treasure? His brother Mime is the only one he must reckon with? And yet he cannot win the golden ring for himself?

It's really very simple, the man in the slouch hat explains. A warrior is coming to conquer the worm and seize the precious. And when the ringbearer Fafner dies, the winner also wins the ring. So the cleverest thing they can do now is warn Fafner of his impending death, because the dragon will probably give up the shiny trinkets to try and save his life. He is going to awaken the beast now, and then the dwarf lord can do the talking.

The former ruler of the Nibelung is utterly confused. Does his arch enemy really no longer begrudge him the ring of power? There is no time to ponder the thought, for Wotan has already woken the monster by yelling and screaming. Fafner wants to know just who is making the wild suggestion: His ongoing existence in exchange for the hoard? Alberich calls into the cave that a hero is marching towards it, bent on the giant's destruction. The warrior's sole interest is the magic ring. If Fafner gave him, Alberich, the ring as a reward, he might be able to avert the fatal battle. Then Fafner could keep the rest of the gold and grow old in peace.

Fafner yawns, obviously bored. His stomach is empty, so he awaits the boy fighter with great appetite. As for the dwarf's grand offer: *"Here I lie and here I hold; let me sleep!"* The wanderer laughs. Well, Lord Alberich, that deal didn't work out, did it? Maybe he can try negotiating with his brother Mime, but otherwise things will happen as they were meant to happen. Says it, mounts his bright steed, and gallops off in the light of a blood-red moon.

The Battle with the Dragon
(SCENE TWO)

Moments later, Mime and Siegfried enter the scene of events. They have been marching through the forest for the better part of the night, and now the young hero, armed with the freshly forged magical sword, sits down to rest at the foot of an old linden tree. He is skeptical: *"Is it here I shall learn fear?"* If he doesn't find what he wants to know in this place, he is going to go on without the annoying gnome.

The blacksmith points to the dark entrance of the cave: This is the lair of the dangerous lindworm. Its maw is so gigantic that it can swallow a man whole with one bite. Its spit contains an extremely poisonous acid, which is able to dissolve flesh and bone. And it also possesses a powerful serpent's tail: *"If he coils it across you and grips you tight, your bones will break like glass."*

Siegfried is not duly impressed by the description. If the giant worm possesses a heart that sits where you find it in any living being, he will thrust his sword into it and be done with the dragon. *"Is that what's called fear?"* He dismisses the dwarf, for he still doesn't feel any of the promised emotion.

Mime insists: Anyone would faint as soon as they saw the monster crawl from its den, causing the ground to tremble under its weight! He will leave the boy to his own devices now, and wait for the victorious one at the nearby spring. That is the spot where the dragon goes to drink when the noon sun heats the forest.

The fighter laughs: If his miserable wannabe father wants to wait at the dragon's watering hole, he will let the beast pass. It can quench both thirst and hunger before he will kill it: *I'll thrust Nothung into his guts only after he's gulped you down too.*

He is thoroughly sick of the dwarf, but the Nibelung goes on about how the boy can always call him for advice, or tell him if he enjoys the experience of fear. Once the battle is over, he will serve up a drink for the victorious one. Siegfried shoos him away with a kick.

The angry gnome mumbles that he hopes the battle will end in a tie—with both parties dead! Then he ducks into the underbrush, waiting to see how it goes. Meanwhile, the belligerent Volsung makes himself comfortable under the linden tree: It's naptime.

*

Wagner could not know at the time that this nap would last all of twelve years. In a letter, the composer describes the interruption of his work: *"I have led my young Siegfried into a beautiful forest solitude, and there have left him under a linden tree, and taken leave of him with heartfelt tears. He will be better off there than elsewhere."*

The composer is facing trouble on various fronts. His negotiations with a music publisher about publishing the score are broken off; the plan falls through. His hopes of staging the *Ring of the Nibelung* in Weimar are dashed. Thus the maestro brings forward a different, one that is even dearer to his heart: *Tristan and Isolde*. After that, he starts writing *The Mastersingers of Nuremberg*, another opera.

But soon, Wagner's life takes several turns for the better: King Ludwig II. of Bavaria comes out of the closet as Wagner's biggest fan. The affluent "fairytale king" would love to experience the entire cycle. The composer digs up the unfinished *Ring* tetralogy, and embarks on finishing it. Work on this project goes quickly, and the 56-year old man finds bliss in his private life, too: On June 6, 1869, only a few months before the completion of the third part, his wife Cosima bears him a son. The couple names their offspring Siegfried, and in thanks for the late heir, the composer gifts his symphonic poem "Siegfried Idyll" to his wife. We will hear that piece of music later in the story. It is counted among the most sophisticated orchestra pieces of the entire *Ring*.

*

Our protagonist is still resting against the trunk of the linden tree. He is glad that, thanks to the dwarf's confession, he finally knows that they are not related. The offspring of the gnome would have to look more like him: *Exactly as ugly, grizzled and grey, stunted and misshapen, hunchbacked and hobbling, with drooping ears and bleary eyes.* Siegfried knows that he looks nothing like that, for he once saw his image in the water of a brook. He looks like a storybook Germanic hero with his curly blond hair. Right now, the fine young man is completely at home in the aromatic fir forest, cheerfully greeting the dawning new day. The orchestra is waving its web of sounds around the scene.

In shimmering eighth and sixteenth notes, Siegfried dreams of his real parents. His father would have looked exactly like him, he is confident, but what about his mother? He has never seen a human woman, so he can only imagine her by comparing her with what he knows: *Like the roe-deer's surely shone her soft lustrous eyes, but far more lovely!* But then he wonders whether all mothers must die after giving birth to a son. He is ignorant of some of the facts of life, and the thought saddens him. With a sigh, he stretches out on the soft ground.

The sounds of the forest enchant him. The strings whisper and breathe, murmur and susurrate. The song of a bird captivates the young man. Can the little flying friend tell him something about his mom? He remembers that Mime told him once that it was possible to understand the language of birds. Siegfried plucks a piece of reed from the underbrush, and uses Nothung to carve it into a flute. But the music he coaxes from the makeshift instrument—down in the pit, a player abuses his English horn—displease the feathered virtuoso on the bough above him. Siegfried throws away the flute and pick up his horn. This noisemaker is more to his own liking, so he blows into it with full steam.

This time he does not lure a bear to his side to keep him company, but a monstrous lindworm. The colossus emerges between the bushes, breathing fire and brimstone, slowly rolling towards the fearless hero, who greets him cheerfully: *Ha ha! So my strains have roused something lovely! You'd make me a pretty playmate!*

Fafner the dragon asks who the loudmouth is. The swordbearer rejoices: An animal that speaks! He can surely learn a thing or two from this beast, preferably what fear is. If the dragon can't teach him that, he will kill him. The monster laughs at the bold challenge. *"I wanted a drink: now I've also found food!"* He opens his enormous mouth and shows off his many point teeth.

As is customary, the parties prelude the battle by heaping insults and scorn upon each other. The young man scoffs that Fafner is graced with a "*delicious maw,*" which needs stuffing and shutting. The dragon answers by menacingly raising his murderous tail. Siegfried says he doesn't like the prospect of being devoured by such an ugly beast, so the monster had better perish ASAP!

And then the antagonists attack each other. The giant worm breathes poison from his nostrils, burying the scene in an obnoxious fog. His challenger evades him with a quick jump to the side. When the dragon tries to crush him with his enormous tail, the hero reacts quick as lightning: He hacks off a piece of the tail, and Fafner cries out in pain. He rears up to throw his entire weight down on the smaller opponent. But Siegfried realizes that this is his chance: He thrusts Nothung into the spot where he guesses the dragon's heart. The sword goes all the way into the monster's chest, up to the hilt. With a mighty groan, his gigantic adversary collapses on the ground.

The fatally wounded dragon wants to know who the bold youngster is. He suspects that the boy was incited by someone else: *Your brain did not conceive what you have carried out.*

Young Siegfried doesn't really know who he is, so he explains his deed by saying that the worm irritated him. The dying beast wheezes that the wannabe warrior has killed the last of the giants. He tells him that he murdered his own brother, all because of the accursed gold they were given by the gods. He guarded these treasures for years in this dragon shape, and now his conqueror had better watch out, because this story would most likely end badly.

The giant is in his death throes, when his assailant asks whether Fafner can tell him anything about his ancestry; he only knows that his name is Siegfried. On his final breath, the giant repeats the name with a sigh. Then he is dead.

The hero pulls Nothung from his chest. Blood spurts from the wound and splashes his body. The dragon's juices burn like fire on Siegfried's skin. Even his fingers are covered in blood, and when he licks them, he suddenly thinks that the birds are talking to him. And really, drinking the dragon's life blood enables him to understand the singsong of the feathered friend from before. The bird observed the entire battle from his box seat in the branches of the linden tree.

Rejoicing in his register of coloratura, the forest bird tells him about the treasure of the Nibelung, which is his due as the winner of the fight. The bird recommends that he take the magic helmet, because it may come in handy if he wanted to "*perform wondrous deeds.*" And if he took the golden ring, "*it would make him ruler of the world!*" Fafner's killer thanks the little friend for the useful advice, before marching into the cave to grab the things he was told to grab.

Thus ends the most famous battle in the world of the opera. The last of the giants lies dead. The dragonslayer is heir to the hoard. After Alberich, Wotan and Fafner, young hero Siegfried, grandson of the father of the gods, becomes Lord of the Ring, without even guessing its significance. But even though he fought a magnificent monster, he still hasn't learned what fear is.

The Ring Claims its Next Victim
(SCENE THREE)

As soon as the giant dragon has exhaled for the last time, Mime crawls out from his hiding place in the shadow of the tall firs. He gingerly checks if Fafner is really dead, before turning to follow Siegfried into the cave. But just then, his brother Alberich jumps out from his cover, hissing and snarling. Does the blacksmith want to steal his gold? Mime says that the gold belongs to him now, for two reasons: first of all he was the one who forged the magic helmet that enables its wearer to shift into anything he wants, and second he also raised the boy who just killed the monster. His brother lost the treasure, but he just won it by patience and cleverness.

Alberich dismisses this argument, countering with one of Wagner's beloved alliteration clusters: *For rearing the boy does the stingy, shabby slave coolly and brazenly claim to be made king?* (The effect is much stronger in German original, where most of the words in this question start with a "k," creating the effect of an angry spitting out of words.)

Anyway, Alberich thinks that he has much more right to wear the ring than his measly brother. The wily blacksmith professes his readiness for a compromise: How about Alberich keep the ring, while Mime takes the magic helmet. That way, the loot will be shared fairly. Sharing? Handing his brother the helmet? Alberich would never be in peace! No, Mime mustn't take even a single piece of gold from the hoard.

Now the blacksmith gets angry, too. Well, if Alberich is that greedy, he won't get anything, for Mime has Siegfried on his side. He will tell him to use Nothung to beat some sense into his brother, oh yes! On the cue, the dragonslayer steps out from the cave. He didn't bring a bunch of glittering trinkets however: The only things he picked from the vast treasure are the helmet and the ring. The two greedy observers are stunned. Mime teases his brother to ask Siegfried to give him the ring as a gift; he intends to win it with wiles.

Meanwhile Siegfried studies the two items the bird told him to pick from the treasure. Nice enough, but he still hasn't learned what fear is. Once again, the orchestra accompanies the scene with beautifully woven melodies. Then Siegfried's feathered friend comes tweeting, congratulating, but also warning him: The dwarf is a scammer, but if Siegfried listens closely to his prattle, he will be able to read the swindler's thoughts. Imbibing dragon's blood has given him more than the ability to understand birds; it has made him almost omniscient!

And really, the young fighter can hear what his mentor really has in store for him. Mime is worried that the wanderer will appear and coax the ring from him. He hast to prevent that and be quicker. The gnome greets the hero by asking whether he has finally learned what fear is. Siegfried shakes his head, nope. The dragon may have been vicious, but he feels sorry for its death. The person that incited him to slaughter it is a much worse character, and should not be alive.

Mime thinks to himself: *What I desired of you you have done: now all I need is to steal the spoils from you.* The dwarf sings his musings as asides, but due to the dragon's blood he drank,

Siegfried understands them anyway, as does the audience. He has become a thought-reader. Now he learns that the potion his foster-father brewed is going to poison him. The gnome hops around like Rumpelstiltskin, eager to have Siegfried sleeping and defenseless, so he can take the loot from him. He is aware that the boy would still be a danger to him, even if he wore the ring, so he intends to kill him as soon as he falls asleep: *So with the sword that you made so sharp I'll just hack off the boy's head: then I shall have peace and the ring too!*

He pours the sleeping potion into a drinking horn and presses him to drink. But Siegfried has had enough; he kills the dwarf with one blow of his sword. Alberich welcomes his brother's death with a laugh, staying put for now. Siegfried carries the dead gnome to the cave and throws him in. Then he rolls Fafner's huge corpse in front of the entrance, sealing it off.

Tired from all the bloodshed, he lies down in the shade of the tree again. He just slaughtered the only companion he ever had; now he feels very much alone. Maybe the forest bird wants to be his friend? Maybe it can even tell him how to go on, where to go from here?

The little bird sings to him in a sugar-sweet soprano: He knows of a wonderful woman that sleeps up on a high rock, surrounded by fire. If a hero manages to march through the flames, the bride will wake up. Her name is Brünnhilde, and no coward could ever hope to win her. Only a man who doesn't know what fear is might do that.

That sounds like an adventure to Siegfried's liking. He wasn't afraid of the fire-breathing dragon, but maybe a fiery lady could show him what fear is. He bids the bird show him the way; he will follow wherever his new friend flies.

ACT THREE

Strife at Valkyrie Rock
(PRELUDE)

Just like the two acts before, the third one is introduced by an orchestral prelude. This time, the musicians start out in a lively four-four time. In a mere two minutes, the music reminds us of all the things that have already happened: from the insouciant play of the Rhine daughters to Alberich's theft of the Rhinegold, from the curse of the ring to Siegfried's victory over Fafner. The location is in the vicinity of Valkyrie rock, wither Brünnhilde was banned by her father Wotan twenty years ago, and surrounded by a ring of fire. The music becomes more fervid, conjuring a storm, thunder and lightning. The violinists make their horsehair bows smolder with intensity, while the brass players push the last bit of air from their lungs. The percussionists bang and clang till their biceps crunch. Whenever the forces of nature bluster like that in the firmament, they herald the appearance of Wotan.

Wotan Determines his End
(SCENE ONE)

A figure in a long cloak and a slouch hat raises a fuss in front of a cave at the foot of the rock. This is the disguise Wotan uses when he roams the earth. In his powerful bass, he demands to speak to Erda, who is lying in a "*brooding sleep,*" pondering the ways of the world and its future. He calls her "*Wala,*" which means soothsayer, or fortune teller.

The seer is loath to be woken from her sleep, but Wotan flatters her, telling her that no one is more knowledgeable than her: *To you is known what the depths hide, what links mountain and valley, air and water. Wherever life exists, your breath stirs: Wherever brains brood, your mind is involved.* He has called her from her slumber because he needs her advice.

The primeval world sage is annoyed by the troublemaker's visit. Why doesn't he ask the Norns, the weird sisters (from Germanic *wyrd* = fate), who sit guard while she sleeps. They spin the rope that holds the fate of the earth as well as its subjects. The old slouch hat knows all that, but insists that he needs Erda's advice: The three Norns weave the thread of fate on Erda's behalf, but they cannot change or influence events. What he needs to know however, is "*how to hold back a rolling wheel.*" The god wants to interfere with the coming events, wants to prevent the prophesied end of his dynasty. But he doesn't know how.

The earth mother is sick of always having to deal with the deeds of men. Why doesn't he ask their mutual daughter, the wish-maiden that she bore him? The girl is bold and wise enough to give him advice.

The wanderer doesn't like to be reminded of Brünnhilde. She defied her father in just that moment when he had to force himself to do something he balked at. The stubborn Valkyrie dared accomplish that which he had wanted to do, but couldn't. He banished her up on that rock, sent her into a comatose sleep. How can he ask her for advice now?

Music represents the time Erda needs to think this over, and then she shakes her expert head. Her own child was sent into a coma while her mother was sleeping? And now the one who set all this chaos in motion is angry because his plans are being actualized with all due consequence? The alleged keeper of law, the steward of the earth, has actually been ruling by false oath? The world has obviously turned wild in her absence, which makes her want to go right back to bed: "*Sleep seal up my wisdom!*"

But Wotan doesn't want to let her go. After all, she presaged the end of his power by evoking the twilight of the gods. During their night together, when they begot Brünnhilde, Erda told him that Alberich sired a son, too. The Nibelung plans to win back the ring with the help of that son, and if he succeeds, he will use the ring's power to mobilize a hellish army against Walhall. As chief god, this is his biggest concern.

The soothsayer merely shakes her head again. Wotan's reign has run its course; his days at the helm of the worlds are numbered. He has degenerated into a restless wanderer, and his spell is no longer working on her. He should leave her be now. And with those harsh words, she vanishes for good.

The wanderer's blood pressure shoots through the roof at her words. The choleric god snaps back that she, too, isn't all she's cracked up to be. Her "*earth-mother's wisdom*" is waning, whereas Wotan's will is still governing the course of events. He is still the "*father of the storms,*" and as such he will gladly execute now what he once decided "*in the wild anguish of dissension.*"

While he was plagued with disgust when he envisioned the Nibelung as the next ruler of the world, he now elects his heir freely: He chooses to bequeath his position to the "*valiant Volsung,*" because Siegfried won the magic ring without his assistance. He knows neither envy nor fear, which is why Alberich's curse cannot harm him. The hero will awaken their daughter Brünnhilde, and she will know how to save the world. Yes, he says, *to the ever-young the god gladly yields.*

Erda can go back to sleep and watch the twilight of the gods in her dreams. For all he cares, she may descend into her catacombs and never wake up again!

Wotan's Power Shatters
(SCENE TWO)

While Erda pulls the covers over her earth mother ears, the forest bird is fluttering towards the rock, young Siegfried in tow. But when the birdie spies the wanderer, it is frightened and disappears. The dragonslayer watches as it flies away, deciding that he needs to find his way on his own. And then Wotan steps in his way.

The young man is surprised by the sudden apparition in his path. Does the man by any chance know where the fire-ringed mountain with the sleeping woman is located? The old guy in the cloak has a few questions in return: Who advised him to look for a rock and desire a woman anyway? The warrior tells him about the Songbird. But how could he understand a Bird's singsong? Well, he drank the warm blood of the dragon: *Scarcely had its wetness stung my tongue then I understood bird-talk.*

And who incited him to slaughter the dragon? Siegfried tells him of Mime, who failed to teach him fear, despite his promise that he would. But it was the worm himself who antagonized him by opening his maw, threatening to devour him. Wotan wants to understand every detail: Who forged the sword that was hard and sharp enough to slay the monstrous beast? The boy does not hold back; he tells him that he had to do it himself, because the dwarf blacksmith was unable to. He isn't interested in knowing who created the pieces of the original sword however. All he knows is that these pieces were worthless until he re-formed them into a sword.

With a friendly laugh, Wotan agrees: "*I think so too.*" Siegfried, who has no experience in polite conversation, feels ridiculed. He's had enough of the old guy with the many questions: *If you can show me my way, say so: if you can't, hold your tongue!* The wanderer demands that the youngster be more respectful of his age, but the nature boy is in the midst of his rebellious phase. All his life, the old fart Mime has been in his way, pestering him until he finally felled him with one hard blow. So the old slouch hat had better not block his path, or else he might share the blacksmith's fate. Anyway, what has the man got to hide with his wide-brimmed hat covering his eyes? Did he lose one eye when he got into someone's way? He could lose the second one today. The boy demands that he show him the way to the rock, "*or I'll chase you off!*"

Wotan sounds all but sentimental when he muses that the boy wouldn't insult him like that if only he knew him. He doesn't want to challenge him, but Siegfried doesn't care what the crone wants or doesn't want. He only desires to know how to find the woman his birdie friend told him about. So the "*obstinate dolt*" should step aside and let him pass. But no, Wotan shakes his head and declares that he is the guardian of the rock. His power binds the "*sleeping maiden*" with an ocean of fire that will burn anyone who approaches her. He doesn't want anyone to conquer the woman, because: *he who wakes her, he who wins her, deprives me of my power forever!* He points to the top with his spear. A crackling fire can be seen up there. If the boy was to climb the mountain, the flames would devour him.

The hero pushes the old man aside, claiming: *I must go there, to the burning heart of the blaze, to Brünnhilde!* But Wotan still won't give in; he blocks Siegfried's path with his spear. Proudly he warns the younger one that its shaft has already broken the mighty sword once before, and it will break it once again today. Even though he had accepted the imminent course of events, he is suddenly seized by jealousy, and doesn't want Siegfried to have his favorite daughter. At this last moment, he tries to stop what cannot be stopped anymore.

Siegfried on the other hand is reminded of the story Mime told him: Is this the spear that destroyed Nothung? That would mean that he's come face to face with his father's worst enemy! This is the man who rendered his sire defenseless, thus sending him to his doom! His blood boils, and he wants to avenge his dead dad, break the damned weapon. He swings Nothung, and the sword shatters the spear in one blow. A flash of lightning erupts from it. Thunder rumbles, and then the orchestra falls silent. The old guy picks up the pieces and finally moves aside: *"Forward then! I cannot stop you!"*

The chief god vanishes in the dark. His reign is over; the spear that governed the fortunes of the world is destroyed. Thus the contracts which have been carved into it have become void. The end of the gods is dawning. Wotan flees to Walhall, entrenching himself behind his monitor to watch the unfolding of events. He won't show his face again in the rest of the story. Begone, Wotan, begone!

The further course of events is now in the hands of his grandson Siegfried. The boy blows his horn and jumps right into the fire, yelling "*Hoho!*" and "*Hahi!*" He storms through the sea of flame, ascending to the top of Valkyrie rock. Ready to conquer his first woman.

The Lady in the Ocean of Fire
(SCENE THREE)

Siegfried succeeds: Unharmed by the tongues of flame, he steps through the ring of fire (cue Johnny Cash now, if you haven't done so before), and emerges on a plateau bathed in sunlight. Under a fir, a war horse is resting in a deep slumber. It's Grane. Next to the horse, an armored figure is dreaming, protective helmet still on its head, covered with a heavy shield. The hero believes the sleeper is a knight. He wants to relieve the man in his uncomfortable sleep, so he takes off the helmet. He is surprised to see long, wavy hair spill out. This seems to be a handsome knight. He takes off the cuirass, cautiously cutting off the mailed circles with his sword.

And all of a sudden, the fearless boy is scared: "*That's no man!*" Brünnhilde lies before him in her white undergarment. The youngster senses that this might be a woman, but he can't be sure, for it is the very first female human he encounters. So far, he has only met a wrinkly dwarf, a giant dragon, and an old wanderer in his life. There haven't been any women. He gets so anxious about the being that sleeps before his eyes that he calls for his mommy. Siegfried wants to awaken the creature, but he is afraid of her gaze. His hand trembles, his bravery has left him. Yes, he is scared: A defenseless woman finally teaches him what fear is. Neither deceitful dwarves nor fiery dragons could do it, but the allure of the female form floors him completely.

Vigorously he tries to shake her from her slumber, but she doesn't react. Alright then, it's win-or-bust, do-or-die: He presses her close, ready to kiss her. The text has him gush: *Then I will suck life from those sweetest lips, though I die in doing so.*

Yes, that magic works; the *"wondrous woman"* finally wakes up. The boy kneels next to her, spellbound. She asks who woke her, and he introduces himself. His name is Siegfried; he came through the fire and took off her armor. Brünnhilde praises the gods, the world and the earth, jubilant that her long sleep has finally ended and she is awake again. In her bright soprano, the former Valkyrie makes it clear that she has been waiting for her prince for many years. He is her *"Waker to life, conquering light, joy of the world."* She loved him even before he was conceived, let alone born.

In her female logic, she is wise and knowing because of her love for him. She has always loved the *"conquering light,"* protecting him despite Wotan's changed order, because she knew what the god really wanted. Siegfried doesn't understand a word of what she is saying: *"Its sense seems strange to me."* But that doesn't matter, for he likes what he sees. Entranced, he stares at the half-naked woman in her underwear. She senses the desire in his gaze, lamenting that without her cuirass, she is a defenseless, sad maiden.

The fighter who went through the fire for her now wants his reward: *O woman, now quench those flames! Still the seething fire!* He grabs her, but she evades his grasp with a yelp. She fears the loss of her virginity. No god ever tried to approach her like this, and even the undead heroes in Walhall used to bow shyly before her. The one who awoke her has already injured her by breaking her defensive armor. She no longer is the Valkyrie Brünnhilde! The young man can hardly contain himself any longer, gripped by a new heat: *"Awaken, be my woman!"* She just told him she has always loved him, so why doesn't she show it now?!

The Valkyrie explains that she meant "love" more in a platonic sense. The "*laughing hero*" should let her go; no touching, no raping with his "*overwhelming force.*" He tries sweet-talking her into intercourse: *"Be mine, be mine, be mine!"* He sings in silvery notes, wooing her with his slippery arguments. If she had been his for all of this time, why can't she be his now? And if she wants to be his from now on forever, this would be the perfect moment to show him a little love. The lady backs down. Doesn't he feel that her gaze is already devouring him, that her arm is embracing him, her blood is rising to meet him? *"Siegfried, do you not fear, do you not fear this wild, passionate woman?"*

All bark and nor bite, as the saying goes. Siegfried is starting to be scared again; he cannot deal with this much libido. Therefore the lady makes short shrift of the issue, grabbing his young body "*in the highest exultation of love,*" as Wagner's stage direction says. She is beyond caring. May "*Walhall's glittering world*" crumble to ashes; may the glory of the gods come to its end. The Norns shall rip apart the rope with its interwoven runes, the twilight of the gods shall dawn, and the night of destruction shall be near. Come what may, all she cares about now is the young fighter's body, brimming with unused testosterone: *"Radiant love, laughing death!"*

Young Siegfried gets carried away now, too. He overcomes his trepidation, tears off his clothes, and pushes himself on the panting Brünnhilde. He professes that she will always be his, that she is his one and only. He echoes her cry of lust in a wild frenzy, resulting in a frantic duet: *"Radiant love, laughing death!"*

Every time the action heats up in such a way that it might bring youth protection to the scene, the light is extinguished. It's time for that again now. The dragonslayer has finally learned fear during the first blind date of his life. The ring of the Nibelung on his finger and the Valkyrie in his arms, he rolls around on the dusty floor of the stage. This opera imposes no restrictions on the reproductive drive. The abrupt onset of applause is the only thing that interrupts the lovers' tryst. It entices them to reappear in front of the curtain, ready to accept the audience's ovations hand in hand.

All's Well that Ends Well?

In this part of the tetralogy, the magic ring has changed its owner again. It now belongs to the man who defeated Fafner. Will Siegfried also succumb to the deadly curse which the Nibelung Alberich placed on the ring?

Will Brünnhilde and her lover live happily ever after, or will there be conflict in their brand-new relationship? The age difference between the two is vast, after all: She was sent into her slumber by her father, when Siegfried hadn't even been born. The boy still has his whole life before him; he will probably meet other women ...

And what is Alberich going to do? He is still lying in wait for an opportunity to strike. The dwarf lord did the same thing Wotan did: He sired a son that should help him seize the ring at some point; the boy's name is Hagen. Is he a danger, too? And then there is the question of the downfall of the race of the gods: Can it be stopped, despite the dark prophesy of the soothsayer Erda? Or maybe the Rhine daughter will get their gold back, and everything turns out for the best?

The fourth and last part of *The Ring of the Nibelung* will tell us how the epic tale ends. Its title gives away that we are in for a gigantic showdown, for it is called "Twilight of the Gods."

TWILIGHT OF THE GODS

Third day of the scenic festival *The Ring of the Nibelung*

First performance:
Bayreuth, Festspielhaus
August 17, 1876

Characters in "Twilight of the Gods"

Siegfried, a young hero looking for adventure, newly in love.
Gunther, cheerless king of the Gibichung, on the lookout for an awesome woman.
Hagen, Alberich's sinister son, Gunther's half-brother, commander-in-chief of the Gibichung.
Alberich, former lord of the Nibelung, hopes to win the ring for himself with Hagen's help.
Gutrune, Gunther's sister, dreams of a lover.
Brünnhilde, Wotan's daughter and formerly his favorite Valkyrie, sold off by her beloved Siegfried under the influence of drugs.
Waltraute, Brünnhilde's sister, Valkyrie in Wotan's service.
Urd (past), Werrdandi (present) and Skuld (future), Norns, three ladies that spin the thread of fate, on which the world's fortunes hang.
Woglinde, Wellgunde and Flosshilde, Rhine daughters who want their stolen gold back at any cost.
Gibichung, men and women that form king Gunther's retinue and act as choir.

Brünnhilde Receives the Ring
(PRELUDE)

The story of the magical ring that enslaves and oppresses the world reaches its climax in this last chapter of the greatest epos of music history. The "*Twilight*" begins with a brief orchestral prelude, too, which sums up the events so far, painting a sinister, ominous picture. Employing his typical technique of repeating motifs, Wagner alludes to several stations of the tragedy as presented so far. The swelling of the Rhine echoes up, as well as the Rhine daughters' calls for the ring that Alberich forged from their gold. We hear Siegfried awaken Brünnhilde from her sleep again, and then we are reminded of the primeval world mother Erda's prophecy of the end of the reign of the gods. Wagner achieves this by interweaving nature motifs into the carpet of sound.

The third part of the saga ended on the rock whither Wotan had once banished his favorite daughter and Valkyrie Brünnhilde for her disobedience. Siegfried had braved the ring of fire around her, woken her from her comatose sleep, and fallen in love with her.

Part IV of the saga-like drama begins with a warning and a raised index finger, because it doesn't portray the young lovers' bliss, presaging the further course of events instead. Three ancient old ladies are working on a seemingly endless rope: These are the restlessly laboring Norns.

Wagner's Norns are mythical characters, dependent goddesses of fate that spin the thread of events and weave it into something greater; the big picture. Contrary to their mother Erda however, these demigoddesses don't have any prophetic or visionary abilities. They don't govern fate, but rather try to keep things together with their Norn rope. They expound on what was, what is, and what will be, telling the story from their point of view—and we listen to them, spellbound and curious what will happen next …

Originally the three weaver woman fixed the rope of fate on the trunk of the world ash tree Yggdrasil. But then Wotan injured the ancient tree, when he fashioned his spear from one of its sturdy branches. In the course of time, the wooden giant suffered from the wound Wotan had hewn, until it withered. A spring that had sprung from the maltreated tree ran dry, "*melancholy of mind*," as the contralto Urd, Norn of the past, sings. Since that time, the ash tree is no longer suited to hold the rope. They then used a fir tree from the rock of fate, but it also fails to keep the rope taut.

Werrdandi, the Norn of the present, therefore tries to loop the rope around a boulder. In her mezzo-soprano, she recounts how Siegfried's sword made Wotan's spear splinter. Upon that event, the chief god ordered the heroes of Walhall to fell the world tree and stack its wood around the stronghold of the gods.

Skuld, the Norn of the future, can already see the bonfire blaze. In her clear soprano she describes the palace that Fasolt and Fafner built, home to the gods and the army of undead collected by the Valkyries, devoured by flames. This seals the end of the gods, the impending twilight that the Old Norse sagas call *Ragnarök*.

Is Wotan's mansion really already aflame? Or is the fiery glow that the Norns see nothing but Loge's aura? Wotan tamed the god of light with the help of his spear, in whose shaft he carved a rune spell to do so. He has already kindled one of the splinters of the formerly invincible weapon at Loge's chest.

This way, he is in possession of a matchstick with which he can set fire to the ash wood any time he wants. The Great Fire seems about to happen.

The Norns do what they can to keep their rope taut. But the ash tree lies felled on the ground, the fir tree groans tiredly, and the boulder chafes the rope. To make matters worse, the evil curse of the Nibelung is corroding the web of fate in the background. Alberich's avenging execration is gnawing at the net, and that proves too much: The rope is torn in two under the extreme strain!

The Norns have become obsolete. From now on, they will ignore the fortunes of the world, because their wisdom is no longer needed. The destruction of nature, the hubris of the gods, and the malice of the dwarves bring about the earth's downfall. The three old ladies step aside. They disappear into the bowels of the earth to join their mother Erda.

Humankind will be left to its own devices; anarchy and chaos are going to reign. The era in which primeval mothers and goddesses governed their fate is over. The population of the earth is entering an as yet unknown phase: From the primordial ooze a new race emerges; free people, in charge of their own destiny. And at this point, the review the Norns have given the audience comes to an end.

Siegfried and Brünnhilde have entered the scene. They represent the new species. And even though she is the first partner in his flourishing young life, the feisty lady manages to hold the warrior's attention only for a very short time, despite her comfy old bed. So much for "sex sells." Eager for action (always the same sad tune with these men!), the fighter wants to find new adventures. He is restless to *do* stuff. And the former Valkyrie sees a correspondingly bleak future for herself: She is worried *"that I was too meager a reward for you."* She pleads: *Do not despise the poor creature who can grudge you nothing but give no more!*

As is customary for scenes of farewell between young lovers, endless kisses are exchanged, and meaningless oaths are sworn. Siegfried vows to always love the woman he woke from her deep slumber. She exhorts him not to forget his vows of fidelity. As a token of his loyalty, the dragonslayer gives her the ring he took from Fafner's hoard. She accepts the piece of jewelry, knowing as little of its real significance as does: Nothing. In exchange for the pretty ring, she gives him her charger Grane.

Excited, the fighter mounts the wonderful horse, proclaiming that from now on, he shall call himself *"Brünnhilde's arm"* instead of Siegfried. This pleases the lady, who can still feel the sting of Cupid's arrow. She feels that they are true soulmates, and calls upon the gods to rejoice in the *"dedicated pair,"* which is now joined in inseparable ways. Rapturously and repeatedly hailing each other, the *"radiant star"* and the *"victorious light"* (in other words: the ex-Valkyrie and Siegfried) part ways.

Their affair lasted only for a short time. Wagner leaves it to the audience to imagine for how long exactly. Between the awakening of the woman who had been sleeping for decades and Siegfried's departure, the days have probably been short and the nights long. After all, for both of them this has been the first amorous adventure of their lives. In the lonely woods where the young man grew up, he never saw a single woman, let alone have the chance to touch one. The virginal demigoddess on the other hand was busy with transporting fallen warriors from the battlegrounds to Walhall, before being banned by the ring of fire. She was working on her father

Wotan's behalf, and the one time she resisted his order, she was punished with that long sleep on top of the mountain of fate, in the midst of that sea of fire.

The fearless hero ended the comatose years by stepping through the fire to wake her up, alright. But is that enough for a life-long, harmonious relationship, current hormonal surges notwithstanding? And another, maybe more pressing question: What will become of the ring now? Siegfried has no inkling of its ominous powers, nor does he know about the curse Alberich placed on the gold. He could return the treasure to the Rhine daughters it was stolen from, and thus save the earth from the bloody oath of the Nibelung. Instead he gives the piece of jewelry to Brünnhilde, as an engagement gift and a token of his fidelity.

She on the other hand knows exactly what she is now wearing on her finger, this gold band fraught with history. Her father Wotan told her the entire story in the second act of "The Valkyrie." But Brünnhilde has other things on her mind; she isn't interested in saving the world, or at least the gods. She hopes that her lover will return soon.

ACT ONE

Siegfried's Journey on the Rhine
(SCENE ONE)

We are returning to the setting of the "*Rhinegold*," the first chapter of the mysterious saga of the ring of the Nibelung, the banks of the river Rhine. The river literally makes the story flow. Valkyrie rock is not that far away from the mighty stream either.

After taking his leave from Brünnhilde, Siegfried built a boat. Now he is rowing upstream, looking for new adventures. His boatride is accompanied by a wonderful piece of music, rife with a multitude of allusions and quotations from the already familiar motifs. Wagner wrote about this bit: "*There is scarcely a bar in the orchestra which is not developed out of preceding motifs.*" At the same time, the composition bridges the gap between the seemingly carefree world of young love and the shady, dubious world of the Gibichung, where the rowboat is taking the young hero.

In the Gibichung castle, Gunther is wearing the king's crown, for he is the firstborn. The pleasure-loving king likes to eat. He likes it a lot. He is not much into fighting or physical competitions of any kind; his half-brother Hagen is the hatchet man. The general of the royal army is the offspring of an affair between Queen Mum Grimhild and the Nibelung Alberich, who lured her with a bunch of jewelry. Hagen is sly, violent and scheming; and the man who wears the crown tends to follow his advice.

During one of his frequent banquets, the king asks him whether there is anything he can do to increase the fame of the house of Gibichung. Hagen tells him about a woman that could strengthen his royal reputation. This woman is *"the finest in the world."* The musicians play the motif of the ride of the Valkyries, hinting that Hagen is well-informed about recent events. He goes on to explain that said woman lives high on a mountaintop, surrounded by a ring of fire. Only the man who can break through the circles of flames is allowed to woo her. This is the prerogative of someone much tougher than Gunther.

The king wants to know just who this tough guy may be. Hagen tells him about Siegfried, from the clan of the Volsung, the incestuous offspring of the twins Siegmund and Sieglinde. Raised in the forest, he used his *"conquering sword"* to slaughter the dragon that used to guard the Nibelung hoard in front of the cave of envy. This brave deed is the root of his fame.

The king has already heard of the treasure that has the power to make the world bow before its owner, if he knows how to use it. But why does Hagen taunt him with riches he cannot win—Siegfried has already seized both gold and woman, hasn't he?

Alberich's son has plans of his own. Cunningly, he suggests: *If Siegfried brought home the bride to you, could Brünnhilde not be yours?* Gunther starts mulling it over. He paces the big hall in mounting irritation: Why would that valiant warrior woo the woman for *him*?

Again, Hagen has a ready answer. Wouldn't it be a great idea to set up the dragonslayer with their sister Gutrune. She has been pining for a man, but couldn't get one. The ugly maiden steps up, curious and playful: Despite her good breeding, she hasn't managed to win a husband. How is she supposed to ensnare this most glorious hero, who is probably already cajoled and caressed by the prettiest ladies?

Hagen points to a locked cabinet in the background. There the family keeps a mysterious tincture, which has the power of turning even the most reluctant man into a love-struck fool. A love potion with a built-in spell of forgetfulness is ready to be served up. As soon as Siegfried drinks from this brew, he will forget that he has ever seen another woman. He will only have eyes for Gutrune.

King Gunther is thrilled. He praises his mother's infidelity, which has given him this intelligent brother. Gutrune warms to the idea now, too, and wants to see the famed Siegfried as soon as possible. But where can they find and meet him? Again, Hagen knows more than the rest of them. It won't be long until the hero will come and visit the Gibichung in search of a new challenge. And really, surprise, surprise—a horn is sounded from downriver: Siegfried announces his arrival.

Blood Brotherhood
(SCENE TWO)

Hagen goes down to the shore, looking at the water, and spies the boat that is being rowed lustily against the current. It carries the warrior and his great horse. Cheerfully the swarthy man waves the boat ashore: "*Hail Siegfried, dear hero!*" The hero lands, leads his charger ashore, and asks to meet the lord of this realm. Gunther steps towards him and introduces himself.

Eager for action, the dragonslayer swings his beloved sword: "*Now fight with me or be my friend!*" The king is not inclined to meet the cocky youngster in battle, so he welcomes him with exceeding friendliness. Hagen's plan is still fresh on his mind.

Gunther leads Siegfried into his palace, shows him the splendiferous furnishings, and basically kisses his ass. He wants to hand over kingdom and subjects, even himself to the warrior. But Siegfried brushes the offer away; he doesn't want to rule kingdom or people. The only thing he possesses is the sword he forged for himself. He offers his strong arm and his weapon for an alliance with the Gibichung.

Hagen, Alberich's son and intimate, knows every detail of Siegfried's adventurous history. He was put into the world solely to bring his father the ring after all. Thus he would try anything to lay his hands on the magical ring. Sanctimoniously he muses that allegedly, there is a Nibelung hoard that belongs to the young man. Siegfried laughs it off: Cheap trinkets! He left the treasure in the cave where the dragon used to guard it.

The intriguer digs deeper: Didn't he take any part of the treasure at all? Yes, the boy answers, pointing to a skillfully forged net that is hanging from his belt. He took the strange thing, because a forest bird told him to. But he doesn't know what it is.

Hagen can tell him what it is: This is a magic helmet made by a Nibelung. If he put it on, he could take any shape he desired. It also comes in handy if you want to travel to faraway places, like the Star Trck crew with their beaming facility. In the background, the motif of the Nibelung cave, familiar from the "Rhinegold," is sampled, because that is the spot where Alberich once demonstrated his magic transformations.

And that was all he took from the hoard, Hagen wants to know. "*A ring,*" Siegfried adds casually, but in the meantime, the ring graces the hand of a "*wondrous woman.*" And here the elf's son slips, for when he finds his background knowledge confirmed by Siegfried's story, he suddenly mutters that woman's name: "*Brünnhilde!*" Oops. Hagen has given away that he knows more than his innocent-sounding questions suggested.

Gunther saves the situation, declaring that he cannot give anything that is worth as much as the magic helmet, and thus he wants to serve Siegfried without any pay. Hagen hastens to open the door to Gutrune's chamber, and waves her close so she can join the men. The freshly groomed and coiffed princess steps into the light, dressed to the nines. Coquettishly she welcomes the guest, holding out a drinking horn filled to the brim with a refreshing brew. Siegfried takes the drink gladly, thirstily. He drinks to his Brünnhilde's welfare: "*To faithful love!*" That is the last time he is going to remember her for a long while.

As soon as he has emptied the horn, the drug shows its fateful effect. Siegfried forgets everything he knows, first of all his beloved on the mountain of fame. When he sees the shyly giggling princess before him, his testosterone level shoots through the roof—or rather, into his crotch. His blood is boiling; he wants to possess this woman! He immediately asks Gunther what her name is, before taking her hands in his and asking for her hand in marriage. That is how fast things proceed with the help of a little magical potion. On the other hand, the opera's four-and-a-half hours are really long enough as it were …

Lady Gutrune is breathless with yearning: Finally a coveted hero wants to get into her pants, a real man! Because she is a royal child of her time however, she knows her manners.

Courtly, demure and prim; she has it down. But she also swings her hips triumphantly when she retreats into her bedchamber, assured that Hagen's strategy is perfect. Siegfried's horny gaze follows her. That magic potion must have been really potent! She leaves it to the men to fix the price, but she can hardly wait to get the strapping young hero into her bed, and become his wife.

To make conversation in the absence of the most recent object of his affection, Siegfried asks Gunther whether he is betrothed, too. The king becomes very sad when he tells him about a woman he dreams of, but cannot have. Well, can't be that difficult, can it? The spanking-new brother-in-law promises to help if he can. The Gibichung explains that the woman of his dreams lives on the top of a rock that is encircled by flames. Only the man who can walk through that fire may become Brünnhilde's suitor. Siegfried repeats the details as if in a trance, but the insidious potion has done a thorough job: He has really forgotten everything! He jumps up, full of enthusiasm, for that sounds like a task to his taste. For his new friend he would gladly go through the fire! He will win that woman for him, if he can have Gutrune in exchange.

The king beams at him. Of course the valiant man can have his sister. But how does he think he can win the bride for him, Gunther? How can he trick her into accepting him in the end? Young Siegfried is a fast learner: Up until recently, he didn't know what magical powers the Nibelung treasure possessed, but now that Hagen has pointed out the properties of the golden helmet, he knows how to use it: *"By the helmet's trickery I will change my shape to yours."*

Real men don't do things by halves—and oath is needed to seal any deal. The two men graze their arms with their swords, mixing the dripping blood in a drinking horn, which chessmaster Hagen has handed them. Blood brotherhood is supposed to seal their agreement, and then they will speak an oath that will lead to disaster—but ho! Hold the horses; it's not time for that yet. If the alliance is broken, if one of them betrays the other, the oath says, then what is dripping into the horn now shall flow "*in torrents.*" In other words, perjury will lead to capital punishment. Dramatic music and the sound of the kettledrum accompany the pact.

Then they both drink from the mixture, and Hagen smashes the drinking horn in a gesture of affirmation. The blood brothers shake hands, but Siegfried becomes a little suspicious: Why didn't Hagen take part in the ritual, and the pact? He says that his blood would only spoil the drink, because it isn't as pure as theirs. Gunther dismisses the topic, for they have stuff to do.

The blood brothers prepare a boat, ready to set out for the rocky mountain range. The king is supposed to wait overnight in the boat, while the hero will woo the lady in his shape. Both want to get the thing done quickly: Gunther is eager to possess the rock woman Brünnhilde, and Siegfried wants to get into bed with his new flame Gutrune.

The bride-to-be has heard the noise of the men's hasty departure. She comes out of her chamber asking Hagen where the men are off to. Her half-brother kindles the flames of her desire by telling her that Siegfried can hardly wait to get married, which sets her all aflutter with excitement.

The sinister chief-in-command follows the boat with his eyes, as it rushes downstream with the speed of an arrow. Everything happens as he planned it: Siegfried brings home Brünnhilde for Gunther, while unwittingly delivering the magical ring right into his, Hagen's, hands.

He sits down in front of the big hall, guarding the castle in the absence of the king. Accompanied by an ominous, ill-boding tune, Hagen belts out his triumph in his deep bass: *Though you deem him base, you will yet serve the Niblung's son.* Now he's got them all wrapped around his finger; and they are fulfilling his schemes. He, the bastard, will triumph over the "*sons of freedom, cheerful companions.*" The symphonic musical picture that echoes Alberich's curse underscores his dark thoughts.

The Woman on the Rock is Captured
(SCENE THREE)

On top of her lonely rock, Brünnhilde is sitting, gazing wistfully at the ring that Siegfried has left as a love token. She covers the ring in hot kisses, when suddenly she hears a noise. One of her eight sisters is rushing through the air on her charger, wanting to pay a visit to the long-lost sister. Excited to finally see her again, Waltraute comes storming towards her. They haven't spoken in decades.

So Waltraute finally dared breaking her father's ban by visiting her renegade sister! Or has he maybe even changed his mind? After all, event that led to her banishment may be interpreted in different ways. Only her rebellion against her father led to the fulfillment of his legacy: Against his expressed will, she protected Siegfried in his fight against Hunding. As the final result, her disobedience led to her father locking her into that ring of fire on the mountain of fate. But now, she blurts happily, the punishment has brought her bliss, for a glorious hero has won her for his wife, and "*in his love I laugh today in delight.*" Is Waltraute here to share her happiness?

Nope. Her sister has come for a very different reason. She is worried about their father, and about the survival of Walhall. Ever since Wotan banished Brünnhilde to the rock, he has been keeping the Valkyries from collecting new fallen heroes for the gods' stronghold. Instead he has been wandering the world, lonely and restless. Recently he came back from one of his sprees with his spear broken! He said a hero had hewn it to pieces. Afterwards he sent his soldiers into the forest to fell the world ash tree, and then its logs were stacked high around the castle. When that was accomplished, he summoned the council of the gods, and since their meeting, the commander-in-chief has been sitting silently on his throne, not speaking another word.

He spurns Freia's apples of youth, the gods' daily fare, the regular enjoyment of which protects them from mortality. The only thing he still does is send out his two ravens as scouts from time to time. In short, Wotan is melancholic, depressed, and as a consequence, incapable of action—hamstrung! The formerly resplendent deity has turned into a seriously ill man that lacks the will to live. The realm of the sky lord is facing apathy and collapse; at least that is Waltraute's summary of the situation.

The Valkyries begged him to do something; Waltraute herself threw herself into his arms, but Brünnhilde was the only thing on Wotan's mind. Waltraute knows that, because she heard him sigh: *If she would return the ring to the Rhine's daughters in its depths, from the weight of the curse would the gods and the world be freed.* That is why she snuck out to come visit her sister. She mounted her steed and rushed to the mountaintop to plead: Brünnhilde's courage should help her do what she must to end the suffering.

The former Valkyrie is confused. It is difficult to process what her pale sister has just told her; it just sounds wild and muddled. And what exactly does she want from her now? Waltraute points at her jewelry: *The ring on your hand, that is it; hark to my words: for Wotan's sake throw it away!*

Brünnhilde shakes her head. Is her sister out of her mind? Why would she yield Siegfried's love token to the Rhine daughters? Is her father maybe jealous of her happiness? The desperate sister tries to explain the truth about that pretty ring: It's cursed! Terrible calamity clings to the gold; is practically woven into it. In order to end Walhall's misery, she must drown the ring of mischief in the waters of the river, thus returning it to the Rhine daughters.

As the saying goes, love is blind. The woman from the rock refuses to even think about Waltraute's warning and pleading. She spent enough time letting her father use and abuse her, and what good did it do her? He banished her here, duh! Once she even tried to save the world and support Wotan, and that was when he turned away from her.

But now she has fallen in love for the first time in her long life. And the gold that she wears on her finger is a symbol of that love. One glance at the jewelry means more to her than the fortune of any and all of the gods. Waltraute can go and return to their council, for all she cares. Her newfound intimacy is her idol now, so what is it to her if Walhall's swank and pomp will crumble? Her sister must leave now, for she won't get the ring, period.

Wailing and lamenting her sister's stubbornness, Waltraute flies away on her horse. Brünnhilde yells after her never to come back. Siegfried entrusted her with the ring, and thus she will never give it away freely. Her new god is Siegfried!

While Waltraute gallops home in frustration, Brünnhilde hears the sounding of a horn: Her lover is back! She runs towards the sound in expectation, but the man she sees climbing the rock is not the one she was waiting for; it's a complete stranger. And with his coming, the most brutal episode in the events surrounding the Nibelung gold unfolds.

Of course the stranger is really none other than her lover Siegfried, but he is wearing the magic helmet, and thus he looks like Gunther. He introduces himself as the warrior that isn't afraid of the fire, and he has come to take her as his wife. She must follow him now.

Brünnhilde is stunned. Who is this man that accomplished what fate had predetermined for only the strongest of heroes, i.e. Siegfried? Is he even of human origin, or did he come straight from out of hell? The Amazon readies herself for a fight, for she will not give in to another: She is attached to the man that swings Nothung; he is the man she loves, and she is ready to defend that love, and her honor.

The intruder says that his name is Gunther, king of the Gibichung, and that he will make her his queen. She refuses, her voice shrill. The ruffian dismisses her dissent, for he is in a hurry. Nightfall is approaching, so it is time to be wedded. Gunther? She's never even heard the name of this annoying upstart. Hard to believe that he really braved the ring of fire. In any case, she doesn't want him!

She holds out her hand to show him the ring Siegfried gave her, saying that his love token will protect her. If she wears this ring, the attacker cannot force her to be with him, she hisses. *The ring makes me stronger than steel: never shall you steal it from me.* She is bluffing, though, for she doesn't know the actual powers this ring possesses, or that it's magical. For her, it simply represents the love of the man who roused her from her sleep. Therefore she shows the aggressor this token as proof that she is already taken.

Siegfried posing as Gunther laughs to himself, before making short shrift of her defense. A grim wrestling match ensues, which ends when the rough ruffian rips the golden ring from her finger. Now he possesses the treasure and laughs at her, to boot. Brünnhilde collapses, overcome and utterly bewildered. How could this happen? Must have been her father Wotan's jealous doing. Whatever it is, the attacker has triumphed, and now he sends her ahead to her bedroom, in order to spend the night with her there: *"Now grant me your cave!"* Delightful line, isn't it?

Broken and powerless, the once-proud Valkyrie walks towards her bedroom, and the man in disguise marches behind her. The potion's effect is still strong. He doesn't remember his fiancée, whom he won with affection. Brute violence is now his tactic. He swore to his blood brother he would win this woman for him, and so he does.

In order to remain loyal to his new friend Gunther, he places the unsheathed sword between himself and the woman he intends to spend the night with. This way, he wants to remain faithful to his pal, in whose stead he weds the rock woman. Nothung serves as a sort of magical chastity belt, proving that his *"wooing was chaste."* Yeah, right.

The curtain falls. We assume that what happens offstage is the obvious, but again it isn't shown; is left to the audience's imagination. In *"The Valkyrie,"* the stage fell dark at the same moment, when the siblings Siegmund and Sieglinde sank back onto the pillows, ready and willing to consummate the lewdest, most indulgent, most scandalous, and most momentous one-night stand in the history of the opera. Little Siegfried is the product of that unheard-of, unspeakable event. The same passionate Volsung blood rushes through his veins.

The scenes are unquestionably similar. But if we stick to what the libretto says (conspicuously meager the stage directions and text here), Siegfried is not the least bit interested in taking Brünnhilde by force. That is why he emphasizes that he will place Nothung "*chastely*" between him and the bride. The sharp blade is there to prevent any physical contact between the pair.

On the other hand, winning a bride by force would imply the nocturnal consummation of their union—especially if we're talking about the logic of the times in which these wild fellows lived. It requires quite a stretch of the imagination to accept that an ancient macho man braves the ocean of fire, wrestles the desired woman to the ground, drags her off into the sleeping "cave," and then nods off before having sex with her.

Another curious issue is the familiar sword, Nothung. Brünnhilde knows this sword well enough, so would the hero really place it in the bed with them, risking that she sees through his disguise?

Wagner remains vague about it all. He glorifies Siegfried as a "*pure hero*" throughout. A brutal rape would jar with this image. The composer is going to let his protagonist stick to this version of events: In the following act, Siegfried emphasizes that he left the lady untouched in this first night. Let's give him the benefit of the doubt for now.

ACT TWO

The Nibelung's Plan
(SCENE ONE)

So while Siegfried in his Gunther guise is busy doing whatever he is doing up there on Valkyrie rock, the real king of the Gibichung sits in the boat below, waiting to receive his bride. His half-brother Hagen is guarding their castle, but the night is long, and so he takes a nap. In the light of the full moon his father Alberich crawls up from the depths, eager for news. He approaches his son in his dream.

The Nibelung has come to remind his son of his destiny. He was sired for the sole purpose of avenging the black elf for his loss of the Rhinegold. His mother bequeathed him the useful genes for power and courage, so he should be able to fulfill his life task.

Hagen calls his father a "*hateful gnome,*" whose wiles Grimhild succumbed to. He is not grateful for his life, for he feels "*prematurely old, pale and wan.*" Cheerful guys such as Siegfried tend to make him want to puke. The lord of the Nibelung agrees with that sentiment. But he is the type that his son ought to love, for he knows no delight and is burdened with suffering.

He goes on to explain that the times are changing. Wotan, who once upon a time stole the ring from him, has now been defeated by his own kin. The Heavenly One lost his power and primacy to Siegfried, and now the entire clan of the gods is doomed, finished. The chief god is no longer dangerous—he will go down with his tribe.

The somnambulant Hagen asks who inherits the riches of the formerly immortal ones. "*I,*" Alberich replies, and then adds "*and you,*" implicating his hopefully helpful son. As long as Hagen remains devoted to his father, and shares his "*rage and rancor,*" they will inherit the world together.

The Volsung hacked Wotan's spear to pieces, slaughtered the dragon Fafner in battle, and consecutively won the ring. In effect, he vanquished both Walhall and Nibelheim. Even Alberich's curse, which brings lovelessness and death to each ringbearer, has proven ineffective in his case. The fearless hero doesn't know the ring's value, and he hasn't attempted to use its power yet. The Nibelung's only goal now is to destroy Siegfried.

He is already serving me towards his own ruin, Hagen murmurs in his sleep. In the end, he must have known all of this when he wove his sinister web of intrigue. Now he awaits the return of the warrior, the wedded woman, and the magical ring.

Alberich isn't finished with his son. He impresses the importance of getting the ring upon him. He knows that Brünnhilde wears the ring on her finger as a love token. If she advised the Volsung to throw the piece of jewelry into the Rhine, then everything would have been in vain: *Then my gold would be lost and no ruse could ever retrieve it.* Hagen must seize the ring the first chance he gets, whatever the cost. After all, that is his sole purpose in life: avenging the dwarf, winning the ring, scorning the Volsung and Wotan. He must swear that he will do everything it takes.

If your own father tells you that he sired you only to fulfill his stupid schemes, you probably won't be all happy about it. How might Hagen feel? Is he going to obey the man who spawned him? Does the watchman in the moonlight maybe have his own plans? Also, it seems that Alberich doesn't know about the latest turn of events, for by now, Siegfried has taken the ring from Brünnhilde again. In any case, the sleeping son reassures his father that he will seize the ring.

Alberich may be paranoid, but to make sure his son complies with his wishes, he asks for an oath. Hagen vows: *I have sworn it to myself: calm your concern!* This oath is not exactly what the father wanted to hear, so he continues to hammer his request for filial loyalty into his son's subconscious, before he finally vanishes as stealthily as he came.

As the devilish Alberich returns home to his realm of shades, the new day is dawning, and the sun is sending out its first reluctant rays.

Siegfried Returns
(SCENE TWO)

The elf has vanished into the morning mist, and now Siegfried steps out from behind a bush. He takes off the magic helmet and turns into his usual self again. The night at the side of the queen-to-be hasn't left any visible traces.

He finds Hagen and asks where Gutrune is. The elf's son rises, rubs his sleepy eyes. He wants to know how the wooing did go. The dragonslayer tells him that he beamed himself over right from the mountain of fate, and that the couple is following him in the boat.

But did he crack that hard nut Brünnhilde, the military man wants to know. But Siegfried doesn't stoop to answer that;

he wants to embrace his own new bride now. Woken by loud calls, Gutrune steps from her chamber. They greet each other with great enthusiasm. The young fool in love declares that by virtue of his latest deed, he finally won her as his wife.

When Gutrune asks whether the rock woman followed her brother Gunther willingly, Siegfried replies: *"Lightly she was wooed for him."* The fire was not a problem either, because he went through it for Gunther, as arranged, so he could win Gutrune in return for his services. Now the princess wants to know all the details: Did the woman really take him for Gunther? He says yes, Hagen was right; the magic helmet really made him look exactly like her brother. The lady succumbed to Gunther's strength.

Gutrune's jealousy makes her probe further, for what she really wants to know is: *"And she was married to you?"* The young swain may not have much experience with women, but he is not a complete fool either. He senses trouble, so he answers evasively: *Brünnhilde submitted to her husband throughout the bridal night.* He assures her that Siegfried's thoughts were occupied solely with Gutrune the whole time. She believes him, for she can see that the magic potion is still fully in effect.

But Gunther's sister is still piqued that her suitor did share the Valkyrie's bed for a whole night. Siegfried points at his trusted sword, which he says he had placed between himself and the lady. He declares that the rock woman was as far away from him as the north is from the east and west. The Gibichung woman he is with now is the only one he dreams about!

When the mists of the dawning day lay on the top of the mountain, he carried Brünnhilde down to the riverside, quickly switching roles with Gunther, so the king could sail home with his new Bride. He should be here soon and confirm the account. Siegfried is that much earlier because he used the magic helmet to teleport to her side.

Gutrune is thrilled by that much magical power. We should take it with a grain of salt when she says: *Siegfried! Mightiest of men! I am filled with awe of you!* She is probably more horny for him that afraid of his abilities. She also likes to play the part of the admiring female, eager to be taken by the virile male. She's basically coming on to him. One and a half centuries before our time, things are getting steamy!

But first Hagen corroborates at least part of Siegfried's story by announcing that he can already see the sail of the royal boat in the distance. Here come the king and his chosen bride! The princess instructs Hagen to invite all the men, for there will be a double wedding: Gunther will marry Brünnhilde, while Siegfried will marry her, Gutrune. She will invite all the women of her tribe, so that they may share in her happiness.

Hagen Invites a Wedding
(SCENE THREE)

Hagen calls the guests from all around by blowing into his huge bull horn. This horn usually functions as an alarm, calling all men to arms. So from all the corners of the kingdom, war horns answer his call.

In case the choir singers have dozed off in the hours they spent waiting for their cue, these clarion calls will wake them up. This is the only choir scene in the entire *Ring* tetralogy; the rest is owned by the solo singers. So now the choir comes rushing in from the wings, dressed up as Gibichung subjects. A host of heavily armed warriors arrives in front of the castle. Whence does the enemy come? Who is the enemy? Is Gunther under attack?

The chief-in-command calms them down, explaining that he called them here so they can welcome their king with all due pomp and pageant. Gunther has wooed a woman and is bringing her home. The fighters react with irritation. A false alarm? Or did Gunther steal the woman from another tribe, and is now chased by their men? Where are the opponents, where are the pursuers? Did the king fight alone? And if there is neither trouble nor danger, then why were they called?

Hagen explains that the hero Siegfried assisted the king in the dating game. Now the royal couple must be duly celebrated. He tells them to slaughter bulls to sacrifice their blood to Wotan. For the god Froh they are to kill a boar, and for Donner a sturdy buck. And finally Fricka shall have a sacrifice of sheep, so she will bless the union. Instead of killing enemies, they must now murder animals. A soldier like Hagen doesn't care, as long as the blood flows freely.

Once that is done, they are to take their drinking horns and get drunk on mead and wine. Their intoxication will be dedicated to the gods, too, ensuring a good marriage. The warriors laugh at the normally grim Hagen, who suddenly seems to have found his merry side. The choir sings: *The Hawthorn pricks no more; he has been appointed bridal herald.*

Alberich's son doesn't even crack a smile. He tells the men to shut up and receive Gunther's bride Brünnhilde with all due respect. He wants them to be loyal to their new queen, and always ready to avenge her if harm should ever befall her. What sort of harm exactly might he be thinking about here?

Brünnhilde Loses it
(SCENE FOUR)

As told by their leader, the assembled Gibichung men step up for the celebratory welcome at the riverbank. They pull the boat ashore, clang swords and shields together, cheer for the foreign woman and their king.

Gunther leads his acquisition to the castle. She looks more like a chained slave than a blushing bride, however. He introduces her to his people: *Home to the Rhine I bring you Brünnhilde, rarest of women. A nobler wife was never won.* Note the passive voice in the last sentence: He doesn't claim to have won her himself.

The noble Brünnhilde trudges behind her new master with downcast eyes. She seems dazed; still cannot process last night's events. She feels a deep shame. Only when Gunther approaches his sister and the dragonslayer, who stand amongst the Gibichung folk in welcome, she is jolted to her senses: What is that weird king talking about? *Two happy couples I see here on show: Brünnhilde and Gunther, Gutrune and Siegfried!* There he is, her dragonslayer! That is the man she belongs to, not this ridiculous fatso next to her.

What the hell is going on here? The hero doesn't even seem to recognize her. She shrinks back in horror, staring at the man who, just a short while ago, swore to be faithful to her till he died. This is the man who came through the fire to awaken her from her long, long sleep. This guy dedicated love songs to her, belted out hymns in his *heldentenor*. This is the glorious youngster that left her with a priceless engagement ring a.k.a. love token, before he went off to find new adventures. Yes, this is Siegfried, and he is the only man that belongs to her!

But the jerk merely grins at her dumbly. Without batting an eye, he has his arm around another woman, a cow-eyed bitch that wears a similarly dumb, love-struck expression. To make matters worse, the unfaithful ass approaches her now, laughing and welcoming her.

The former Valkyrie is so stunned she can only stutter. *"Siegfried... here...! Gutrune...?"* Sure, the man who completely forgot her says. This is Gunther's lovely sister Gutrune, and I will marry her, while you're going to marry the king. Any problems with that?

The rock woman is about to collapse, ready to faint. When her amnesiac beloved catches her so she doesn't drop to the ground, she whispers: *"Does Siegfried not know me?"* Indeed, he doesn't. The fool is still under the influence of Hagen's witchy potion. He hands her—and thus the problem—over to the king, insisting she belongs to him: *"Gunther, your wife is not well!"* The ruler of the Gibichung demands that she pull herself together and act normal. The dragonslayer agrees and points at the king again, to underline that this is the man she is supposed to look at.

But in that moment, Brünnhilde sees the glint of gold on Siegfried's finger: Why, that is her engagement ring; this thing the faithless lover is wearing! So what kind of crap game are these people playing? Only last night, Gunther wrestled the ring from *her* finger. Siegfried must have gotten or stolen it afterwards from the king. How else could it be in his possession now? But when should this have happened, if the dragonslayer spent the night here at castle Gibichung, waiting for the return of the realm's ruler?

The young fighter looks down at the piece of jewelry. He cannot remember getting engaged to this woman. He mulls it over and decides: He did not receive the ring from the king, no. Of that much he is sure.

The former Valkyrie turns to the ruler. When he "wedded" her, only a few hours ago, he tore the same ring from her finger. Thus it belongs to him, and he needs to demand it back from Siegfried. Gunther breaks into a nervous sweat, afraid he's losing control of the situation. What is the weird woman talking about? What ring? He didn't give Siegfried any precious gold. Period. Let's talk about something else please.

But his uncouth conquest from the mountain of fate has recovered from her initial shock now, and she won't stand for this damned charade. She draws herself up to her full height, snarling at the Gibichung: Well, if that isn't the one, then where is he hiding the ring he took from her?

But the king doesn't know what riles his bride so. He has no idea what happened when Siegfried played his part. His double didn't tell him, so he can only maintain an awkward silence.

Now Brünnhilde loses it completely, because the scales fall from her eyes. Flaring with anger, she points at Siegfried: *Ah! He it was who tore the ring from me: Siegfried, the thieving deceiver!*

What an accusation! The charge of fraud, of deception, of cheating is in the air. The assembled citizens listen closely, and start to speculate loudly about this strange and unexpected turn of events.

Meanwhile, Hagen forges his iron in the fire of this brewing trouble. The intriguer has a detailed plan for laying his hands on the coveted ring, because of course Alberich's son wants the magic ring for himself. Only a short while ago, he made his soldiers swear an oath of loyalty to their queen-to-be, and now he whispers to them from the background: *Now mark carefully this woman's complaint!*

Brünnhilde insists. The ring on Siegfried's hand is the one that was taken from her. She points at King Gunther: It was him! The dragonslayer said he was waiting here at the castle, so how the hell can it be possible that he is now wearing her ring? Murmurs of speculation in the assembly.

Young Siegfried reiterates that he didn't receive the ring from the king. He recounts his version of the story like a man in a trance: The gold was his reward for the battle he fought in front of the cave of envy, when he slaughtered the fearsome dragon Fafner.

Hagen uses the spreading confusion cleverly for his ends, asking Brünnhilde whether she is certain that this is the selfsame ring. For if it is the ring she yielded to Gunther the night before, then doubtlessly it belongs to him, and nobody else. Without waiting for her answer, he acts as judge and jury over the current ringbearer: *Siegfried obtained it by trickery, for which the traitor must atone!*

In a soap opera, the next scene would show a wild catfight, in which the rival ladies would scratch each other's eyes out. Richard Wagner chooses to be more dramatic, meaning that the showdown is protracted, delayed. Brünnhilde appeals to the ultimate authority, the gods. In a strong-voiced solo she asks for their support in her distress. She is mad with anger; she wants revenge. She implores the divine judges to break her heart, so she is enabled to destroy the man who betrayed her so shamefully. The shocked king asks her to tone it down, because he is afraid to lose face before his subjects.

But nobody can stop the maddened woman now. She yells at the assembled tribe: *Know you all: not to him, but to that man there am I married.* With her voice soaring to the high B flat, she points to the hero.

The mob vents its anger. The dragonslayer as the groom of that manic fury? Siegfried instead of Gunther? But he's the chosen husband of their princess Gutrune! Brünnhilde confirms it, still on a furious roll, oh yes: *He wrung from me gratification and love.*

All eyes are of Siegfried. His honor has been publicly challenged. There is hardly a stronger accusation in the code of his times. Is he going to hack the offensive woman to pieces now?

No, the young man remains surprisingly calm. He tries to vindicate himself by recounting his version again: He and the king are blood brothers, and he used his sword Nothung to keep that oath of loyalty, to testify to it. Its sharp blade separated him from the plaintiff, that *"unhappy woman."* For one thing should be clear: If a razor-sharp sword lies between two people, they cannot have sex without suffering grave injuries.

Brünnhilde answers that with scornful laughter. The hero lies! She knows the sharp edge of his weapon, but she also knows its sheath, and that covered the trusted sword, which was leaning upright against the wall of her chamber, while Siegfried was taking her. Which night is she talking about now? Does she describe the night she fell in love with Siegfried, when their brief but passionate love story commenced? Because that night, no sharpened blade was between them; that much is true. Or does she mean last night, when a figure that looked like Gunther attacked her, only to fall asleep peacefully next to her—always assuming that that is what happened?

Yes, it's confusing, and the people present have no idea that the Valkyrie and the dragonslayer had already met a while before all of this chaos, and that they were lovers. They must assume that Siegfried somehow managed to cheat on Gunther by sleeping with his bride, though it's hard to see how and when that could have happened. Hagen, who could clear up a lot of the confusion, keeps his mouth shut. He probably rubs his hands in secret glee.

The king's soldiers speak up. Did that blond impostor break faith or not? Did he dishonor the oath? Did he thus besmirch Gunther's honor? The ruler starts wailing that he is publicly shown up and disgraced, if his future brother-in-law doesn't refute what this blithering woman is saying. And sister Gutrune joins the yammering, asking whether her fiancé was faithless. She demands that he prove that Brünnhilde is lying.

What now? It's a stand-off, his word against hers. The plebs demands a cleansing oath. If Siegfried speaks the purifying oath, the accusation is nil. In a medieval view of law and justice, such a vow serves to clear up an issue that other forms of investigation or atonement cannot solve. The dragonslayer, still under the influence of the oblivion-inducing potion, is ready to swear the oath. He asks for someone to put their weapon against his in the ritual.

All the men present know that their tools stand no chance against the legendary sword Nothung. None of them volunteers, except for Hagen. He raises his spear, so the vow can be made. Siegfried puts his right hand on the weapon and speaks the oath, which will have dire consequences: *Where blade can pierce, you may pierce me; where death can strike, you may strike me, if that woman's accusation is true and I broke faith with my brother.*

Siegfried swears this oath in good conscience. He claims that he hasn't slept with Brünnhilde last night; he merely conquered her for Gunther. His former affair with the lady however has been erased from his consciousness.

Brünnhilde on the other hand feels doubly betrayed by his vow. How can he pretend that he never met her? He could not have forgotten their passionate nights. She rushes forward and pushes his hand away from the spear. Then she proceeds to speak an almost identical oath, venting her boundless anger and frustration. His was a false oath, spoken by a man who broke all his vows. She in turn now dedicates the spear: *I dedicate your dominant power to his downfall! I bless your blade, that it may pierce him.*

The Gibichung subjects are beside themselves. They call upon the weather god Donner to silence the scandal that has erupted here. Siegfried however appeals to Gunther, asking that he let the lying woman rest for a while. Maybe her insane anger will eventually subside. He then calls upon the men to turn away from the shrill yapping of the womenfolk, and to follow him to the banquet table instead. He intends to be extra cheerful today, and he expects everyone to follow his example, if they sanction his union with Gutrune.

Before he takes the princess' arm and strides into the great hall with her, he leans close to the king, whispering to him. He feels even angrier than his blood brother for his bungled camouflage. The magic helmet is obviously flawed, which is why Brünnhilde suddenly seemed to recognize him from last night. Still, he is sure that her wrath will die down, and she will be grateful for her chance to become his queen.

The Murder Conspiracy
(SCENE FIVE)

Brünnhilde is still completely flabbergasted. What ruse and sleight of hand could have gotten her into this situation? All her knowledge seems useless, and the runes that used to protect her are inefficient. Who can help her atone for the shame she endured?

Hagen comes sucking up to her, trying to solicit her trust. He offers his services for the revenge on the traitor. "*On whom?*," Brünnhilde asks. The elf's son states the obvious: "*On Siegfried, who betrayed you.*" The former Valkyrie bursts into laughter. The commander-in-chief wants to face the dragonslayer in battle? Is he joking? The hero would make short shrift of him with a single glance.

Hagen counters that he won't make short shrift of his trusted spear, the one upon which he swore his false oath. But the woman laughs at him again. Stronger weapons are needed to defeat the strongest of the strong.

The elf brushes it aside. Yes, he knows that the drinker of the dragon's blood is invincible, blah blah. But surely she has some advice on how to destroy him anyway? She can only tell him that Siegfried cannot be slain in open battle. He is however vulnerable to attacks from behind, in his back. But because he isn't the type to turn and run away from a fight, the wannabe soldier won't ever see his back.

Hagen is satisfied. He finally knows the warrior's weak spot. "*And there my spear shall strike!*" He approaches Gunther, but the king is still busy lamenting his disgrace, feeling like "*the most wretched of men*" for being shown up in front of his people. Now everyone knows that he didn't woo and win his wife on his own. Can he even remain king under these circumstances? The Valkyrie eagerly turns the knife in his wound: All he did was hide behind the hero's back and then reap the fame of the other one's deeds. The clan of the Gibichung must have sunken really low, to bring forth such a measly coward!

Now Gunther sees red, caught between a rock and a hard place. He is both deceiver and deceived, both traitor and victim of treason. He asks Hagen to reinstate his honor, and while he's at it, to restore their mother's honor, too, for she gave birth to both of them. Black elf junior is very happy with the course the conversation has taken, because now, only blood can wash away the disgrace. Hence there is only one thing to do: Siegfried must die.

The Gibichung ruler is gripped by dread, for that guy is his sworn blood brother! Did Siegfried really break the blood oath? Of course he did, Brünnhilde chimes in. *He betrayed you, and you all have betrayed me!* The death of the worst offender will be sufficient atonement however. The proud woman announces the verdict in shrill tones: *Siegfried shall die to redeem himself and you!*

Gunther is still hesitant, but his half-brother continues to badger him, too. He finally tells him about the significance of the contentious ring, which only death could wrest from Siegfried. The piece of jewelry isn't merely an engagement token, it is the ring of the Nibelung, and possesses tremendous power.

That finally convinces the king. They decide that the warrior must die, even though Gunther finds a moment to consider his sister Gutrune, who should really have a husband. Brünnhilde dismisses his sympathy, claiming that only a spell could have made her man love that other woman. Her jealousy makes her wish Gutrune ill: *"May anguish overcome her!"*

And Hagen already has a cunning plan. The next morning, the men will go hunting together. Eager Siegfried will certainly want to lead the pack, and then he can fall victim to a raging boar. Unfortunate accidents happen easily in the lonely woods, don't they? At least that's what they are going to tell Gutrune. Both Brünnhilde and Gunther like this idea.

Then the demoniac trio seals its strange pact in song. Each of them sings their own tune, but there is consent on the merits of the issue. Siegfried shall, Siegfried must die! First, Gunther wants to whitewash the stain on his honor with the blood of the traitor. Second, Brünnhild calls upon Wotan to hear her oath of revenge. Third, Hagen wants to see *"the handsome hero"* perish, so he can finally seize the coveted ring. He prays to his father Alberich, the devilish Lord of the Nibelung, to watch over him.

Almost like a parody of the agreed-upon execution, the wedding procession of Siegfried and Gutrune passes by in the background. The doomed man is carried past by the Gibichung people on a shield, the princess on a throne seat. Brünnhilde would like to scratch out Gutrune's eyes, but Hagen stops her and pushes her closer to Gunther's side. The cheering subjects lift up the second couple, carrying it to the flower-bedecked sacrificial site. For now, everyone is busy celebrating the double wedding.

ACT THREE

The Death Message from the Rhine
(SCENE ONE)

Siegried is not successful on this morning's hunt. He follows a fat bear, whose trail leads him to the riverbank of the Rhine. The bear is nowhere to be seen, but the Rhine daughters emerge and start frolicking in the water.

We know Woglinde, Wellgunde and Flosshilde from the "Rhinegold," the beginning of the monumental tragedy. They were a bit too flippant about their duty, which was guarding the gold. Alberich managed to steal it from them, and invoked the magic of the treasure by cursing love itself. That initiated the drama we have been witnessing.

In Nibelheim the elf forged the ring of power, with whose enslaving force he wanted to become master of the heavens, the earth, and even hell. But then the chief god Wotan wangled the treasure off him by a ruse. He used it to pay off the giants, who had built the celestial castle Walhall. In his boundless anger, the Nibelung placed a deadly curse on the ring, the effects of which have been swift and extensive: Master builder Fafner slew his brother giant Fasolt, when they argued about the distribution of the payment. The fratricide turned himself into a terrible lindworm. The dragon in turn was slaughtered with the magical sword Nothung by young Siegfried. The fatal ring is now glittering on the hand of the dragonslayer, which may be the reason the three nixies have lured him here.

He watches their splashing water-play with a smile on his face. If the shaggy bear that got away from him was their suitor, he gladly leaves it to them, he says. Woglinde asks what he would give them if they caught the game for him. Well, he hasn't caught anything yet, so what is their price for some tasty meat? *"A gold ring gleams on your finger,"* Wellgunde sings, before all three of them call out: *"Give it to us!"*

Whoa, that seems a little too much. After all, he defeated a giant dragon to get this piece of jewelry, so he deems it worth more than the paws of a bear. Don't be such a cheapskate, the girls tease him. Doesn't he know that a man should always be generous with the wishes of women? The dragonslayer answers that his wife would berate him, if he gave away his possessions like that. The girls take to giggling. What a maleficent wife he must have! Does she beat him? Is he afraid of her rolling pin or frying pan? They taunt him again for his stinginess, before diving underwater. He cannot allow such fishy beings to insult him. Let them have the stupid trinket then! He calls them back: *"Come quickly! I'll give you the ring!"* The water maidens return to the surface, but they have metamorphosed into something else.

Mere moments ago, the beauties seemed to be competing in some "Miss Water" pageant, but now they act more like wise soothsayers. They want to enlighten Siegfried on the disaster that adheres to the ring. If he knew its history, he would be glad to be rid of the heavy burden, they say.

In polyphonic antiphony, the daughters describe the curse Alberich placed on the ring. They prophesy that, just like the lindworm he killed, the hero is doomed, too. He will die today, but there is one way to escape this terrible fate: He must return the hoard to the Rhine, who is its rightful owner. Only the waters of the stream could wash away the deadly curse. Otherwise it has already been woven into the thread of his life by the Norns.

It would have been better if the ladies had kept their mouths shut, because now Siegfried fumes: What, he is supposed to die today? A hero that deems himself invincible is hardly afraid of dying. His magical sword Nothung will tear the rope of fate that the Norns have spun for him. If even a dragon couldn't teach him fear, what else can? In any case, those who prophesy danger for life and limb are certainly not worth the ring. Things might be different if they had offered him a little love (read: sex), for then he would gladly have given them the ring.

The daughters give up their attempt at warning him. They know the end of that story already. The hero may think that he is oh so strong and wise, they sing their swan song, but really he is caught up and blind. He swore to be faithful to Brünnhilde, yet he flouted her. Though he sees the signs of the future, he ignores them. As quickly as he won the love of a woman, he forgot her. Only the damned ring, "*which dooms him to death,*" he seeks to keep at all costs.

Farewell, Siegfried! A proud woman will inherit what he won't give up. She will listen to them, so they intend to swim to meet her instead. Unfazed, the warrior watches them dive under and vanish. He concludes that all women are really the same, in the water as on solid ground. If you don't fall for their sweet talk, they threaten you. And if that doesn't impress you either, you're in for their scolding. And yet he thought these three were quite attractive. If it wasn't for his beloved Gutrune, he would have loved to try and tame himself a Rhine daughter.

Still lost in these charmless musings, he hears the horns of the hunters in the distance. The rest of the Gibichung are finally catching up with him. He blows into his own horn, which was forged by his foster-father Mime, and thus gives away his location.

Siegfried's Death
(SCENE TWO)

Hagen reaches the river first. Siegfried waves the men down to where he is sitting; a good place for a rest. They are carrying provisions, drinking horns and wineskins, and they put down the game they have caught so far. Hagen asks what the hero has bagged. The youngster laughs that he will have to go hungry if they won't share some of their food. The only game he met consisted of three wild water birds, who sang to him that he must die today.

King Gunther is startled, and worries that someone has given their plan away. He throws his half-brother a dark look, but Hagen plays it cool: *That would be a sorry hunt if a lurking beast were to lay low the luckless hunter himself!* But he heard that Siegfried understood the language of birds, and if he can grasp the meaning of the waterfowl's song, it must be true.

The dragonslayer waves a dismissive hand. He has long ceased to pay attention to the twittering and tweeting around him. He hands Gunther his horn, encouraging him to have a drink, for the ruler seems all too melancholy. Gunther says that it looks as if Siegfried's blood is the only liquid that fills the horn. Oh well, the hero laughs it off; then he will mix Gunther's with his, and also feed mother earth. Says it and pours from the king's horn into his own, until it overflows.

But the king's melancholy won't lift. He heaves a sigh, prompting Siegfried to ask Hagen whether it's Brünnhilde who bothers Gunther that much. Hagen shrugs: *"If only he understood her as well as you do birdsong!"* He alludes to the prophesy of the Rhine daughters. But the young warrior gave up his feathered friends once he's heard a woman's song. The dark elf's son pushes him to tell his story, and Siegfried complies.

In a sprawling aria, he sings of his upbringing and adventures, starting with his childhood and Mime, who taught him a blacksmith's craft. The only aim of all the things the grumpy gnome ever taught the boy was to prepare him for slaying a dragon, because that dragon was guarding a vast treasure. All they needed in addition to a slayer was a sharp sword, but the alleged master smith was unable to forge the appropriate weapon. In the end, Siegfried seized the hammer and made his own sword, the trusted Nothung, with which he then killed the dragon.

Something wondrous happened next: The worm's blood on his fingers burned him, so he wanted to lick it off. But as soon as he tasted it, he understood what the birds sang. One of the feathered birdies told him that the cave held a magic helmet, as well as a ring that would make him the ruler of the world.

By now all the men have gathered around the singer to hear the rest of the story. Siegfried recounts how he took the two objects and chatted with the waiting forest bird. It warned him of his foster-father Mime's designs: He wanted to kill him and have the treasure for himself. The Gibichung lean closer, excited to hear what happened next.

The hero glances around the circle of listeners. The stupid blacksmith tried to poison him with a lethal brew, but he was suddenly able to read the rascal's thoughts. Knowing his evil plans, he slaughtered the gnome with his sharp sword.

Hagen interrupts him, offering his wineskin to jog his memory, lest Siegfried forgets parts of his past. Well, the first potion brought him oblivion; let's see what this one will do.

The storyteller goes on: The talking bird congratulated him on being rid of the annoying dwarf, and then told him of a wonderful woman he might want to win. She was supposed to be sleeping on a mountaintop, surrounded by a sea of flame. If he could get through to her, he could awaken himself an impressive bride. And her name was Brünnhilde.

King Gunther starts fidgeting. This part of the biography of his newly-betrothed wife is new to him. He listens breathlessly, as the hero talks about climbing the rock, rushing through the fire, and finding a woman dressed in full-body armor. The forest bird had told him the truth. He freed her from her cuirass, roused her with a bold kiss, and then—*Oh, how ardently was I enfolded in fair Brünnhilde's arms!*

Open-mouthed, the newly-minted husband of the rock woman listens to this outrage. And with this shocking end of the story, two black ravens fly up, cawing. Those are the spies Wotan is still sending out to listen in on the humans. Gloatingly, Hagen asks whether Siegfried understands these scouting birds, too. The hero gives a start and turns his back, to follow the fluttering spies with his eyes.

The elf's son uses this moment of inattention, ramming his spear into the dragonslayer's back, shouting: "*To me they cry revenge!*" His half-brother Gunther interferes, but too late—the young hero is lethally wounded. Siegfried teeters, tries to crush his enemy underneath his shield, but fails and collapses on the ground. "*I have avenged perjury!,*" the murderer thunders at the stunned hunters, pointing at the bloodied corpse.

Well, this is an opera; and it is part of the opera's etiquette to allow the dying to utter some famous last words. Nothing is more theatrical, more dramatic than death, after all. So Siegfried is not quite a corpse yet, but can finally gain some deep insights he couldn't grasp when he was a cocky, reckless fighter. But now he sees the light, one could say.

The spell of oblivion that came with Gutrune's welcome drink is gone. The dying man appeals to his "*holy bride*" Brünnhilde, whom he betrayed. Only now Siegfried realizes what he was because of this woman. He experiences his own awakening in time with his last breath. And before he closes his eyes forever, he sees the image of Brünnhilde.

Driven by tremendous drumbeats, a symphonic poem commences, that is often categorized as a funeral march. But this music is devoid of the typical flavor of a march. It describes the hero's life by way of the different leitmotifs. Accompanied by these immensely tragic sounds, Siegfried's corpse is carried back to the Gibichung castle.

Farewell to the Ring
(SCENE THREE)

Up in the castle, Gutrune is plagued by nightmares. She wakes with a start and starts pacing, from her chamber to the great hall. Did she just hear Siegfried's horn in the distance? Or was that the wild whinny of Grane? Was she woken by Brünnhilde's laughter, whom she saw walking down to the riverside? She presses her ear against the door of the room where her brother's new wife is sleeping, opens the door shyly: The chamber is empty! Then maybe what she saw was not merely a dream?

Just in that moment, Hagen's voice can be heard, calling the sleepers in the castle in his deep bass: *We are bringing home the spoils of the hunt. Hoiho! Hoiho!* The sinister man steps towards his half-sister, asking her to come and greet Siegfried, who has returned home to her. His meanness borders on the perverse.

In the background, the Gibichung are approaching, bearing torches. Gutrune recognizes a lifeless man on the shoulders of the hunters. She is scared: "*What has happened, Hagen?*" The black elf enjoys being the one who tells her that the hero is dead. Never will he blow his horn again; never will he fight or woo any women. Gutrune trembles. What is that supposed to mean? Who is the unfortunate one that the men are carrying in? He callously says it: "*A wild boar's prey, Siegfried, your dead husband.*"

The princess screams, rushes over to the stretcher that carries the corpse. When she recognizes her husband, she collapses on top of him. Gunther pulls her up and wants to hold her, but she pushes him away. Siegfried was slain! *Away, faithless brother, my husband's murderer!*

He washes his hands of the deed. She shouldn't berate him, but Hagen, for he was the damned boar that tore apart the warrior. He curses both perpetrator and deed. Suddenly the focus of unwanted attention and only thinly veiled enmity, the Nibelung's son finally drops his mask: *So be it! But I slew him. I, Hagen, struck him dead.* He killed him with his spear, on which the draonslayer had sworn a false oath. Now he demands what is his according to the "*sacred right of reparation.*" He wants the ring from the dead man's finger.

But Gunther stays his hand. If anyone has a right to take that ring, Siegfried's inheritance, then it is his widow, Gutrune. The commander-in-chief draws his sword. As Alberich's son, it is *his* inheritance, and nobody else's! They fight, and Hagen fells his half-brother, before the men manage to seize him. *"Give the ring here!,"* the murderer yells, grabbing for the gold.

In this moment, the dead man lifts his arm and points threateningly towards the heavens. The witnesses start shrieking in shock; even the toughest soldiers break into a cold sweat. The mythical gesture is supposed to express that Hagen has just been judged as a common murderer by an ordeal, another word for a divine tribunal. The gods, conspicuously absent for a log while, have spoken here.

The general hullaballoo is intensified by the roar of the trombones, which accompany Brünnhilde's reappearance on stage. Even though the demigoddess was excommunicated by her father Wotan, she still possesses enough visionary powers to see though it all, and to know what is needed now. She demands that the men entomb the hero with all due dignity and reverence.

Gutrune tries to take over the proceedings. She claims that Brünnhilde has brought only misery to the house of the Gibichung, that she bewitched the men when she met them. But the Valkyrie silences the princess with a wave of her hand. She knows that she is the one true wife of the hero, because he swore an oath of faith to her before he had ever heard of Gutrune's existence. The princess then merely seduced him.

In spite of her despair and distress, Gutrune realizes that this is the truth. She turns against Hagen, cursing him for recommending the magic potion, which won her Siegfried's affection. Now she knows that the brew made him forget Brünnhilde, his first and true love. The men take a step back, wary of the remaining players in this game. Leaning on his weapons, Hagen stands alone on one side, like a defiant statue.

Solemnly Brünnhilde turns to the men. She orders them to erect a high funeral pyre, on which to cremate Siegfried. They are also to bring his horse, on whose back she will follow the warrior into the flames. In the realm of the dead at least, the woman wants to be united with her beloved Siegfried.

But first she takes farewell of her true love in this realm, belting out another dramatic and tragic aria. He was the purest, even though he betrayed her, because he was loyal to his friend. Nobody swore truer oaths; nobody kept his contracts more faithfully than him. But despite all the oaths and all the contracts, the purest man turned into a traitor, the most loyal man into a deceiver, and the lover became a cheat.

Brünnhilde's swan song rises to become a passionate accusation of her father, the chief god Wotan. She will send home his ravens, who hear everything, and she bids him eternal rest. But her inheritance, the cursed ring, she will return to her wise sisters, the Rhine daughters. She is grateful for their counsel. Once the pyre has burned out, they must retrieve the ring from the ashes, and bury it deep in the riverbed of the Rhine. The fire may cleanse the ring from its curse, so the daughters can then dissolve the forged circle, *"and keep pure the gleaming gold that was disastrously stolen from you."*

The ravens are still circling overhead. She tells them to fly to Walhall and tell their master everything. They shall go past the mountain of fate, where the flames are still burning brightly, commanding Loge, the god of light, to come to Walhall, too. For as soon as the funeral pyre is set on fire, the stronghold of the gods will be set ablaze, too. The end of the gods has come, the prophesied twilight has arrived!

The music is furious as Brünnhilde mounts her magical Horse Grane and jumps into the pyre. She wants to become one with her lover in the fire. The orchestra turns up the volume for the grand finale.

The flames blaze up and devour Siegfried, Brünnhilde and Grane. Then the Rhine swells high, washes across the site of the funeral, and pulls down the ash and remains into the depths. The Rhine daughters ride on the crests of waves. Flosshilde holds up the recaptured ring, rejoicing in its recovery. When Hagen sees the glint of gold on the water, he throws himself into the river, his insanity showing in his maddened cry: "*Keep away from the ring!*"

His father Alberich yearned for their wet embrace in the "*Rhinegold,*" and now Woglinde and Wellgunde are wrapping their arms around Hagen, dragging him down in a vortex. The maidens are exultant: They retrieved the cursed ring of the Nibelung, and they will never give it back.

The earth has been saved, because the power of the Nibelung is gone, overridden. Alberich's brother Mime and his son Hagen have been destroyed. The powerless black elf alone remains, a lord without kingdom. The race of the giants is extinct, for Fafner was their last lord. And even the era of gods and demigods is drawing to an end. Walhall is burning, obliterating Wotan, Fricka, Freia, Donner and Frohh, along with the remaining Valkyrie and their army of undead heroes.

A new era begins; that of the humans. Will this species be able to withstand the lure of gold? Will they lead free and self-determined lives? That is another story. The exciting spectacle around the ring of the Nibelung has shown how hard it is not to succumb to the power of gold and riches, and that selfishness, vanity and intrigue are ugly traits, in gods and people.

The *"Twilight of the Gods"* finishes with downright anthemic sounds. They remind us of the events of the past four nights. Some listeners might feel the goosebumps, when the powerful music fades with the last beat of the kettledrum. For a long moment, silence reigns. And then the audience bursts into redemptive, cathartic applause.

The Author

Wilhelm Ruprecht Frieling is an unconventional German author, publisher and producer. He has published over 40 books, maintains several blogs, promotes all manner of talents, and serves as a consultant for diverse clients. He manages the German-language portal www.literaturzeitschrift.de, functions as a producer of various cultural events, and founded the first German opera blog.

On the web:
Home base:
http://www.RuprechtFrieling.de

Printed in Great Britain
by Amazon